Charting Your Financial Course

RETIREMENT STRATEGIES WITH

GLOBAL WEALTH MANAGEMENT

C. Grant Conness and Andrew M. Costa

with Kevin Haskin

Global Wealth Management

FORT LAUDERDALE, FLORIDA

C. Grant Conness and Andrew M. Costa/
Global Wealth Management
2810 East Oakland Park Blvd.
Ste. 101
Fort Lauderdale, FL 33306
https://askglobalwealth.com/

Book Layout ©2013 BookDesignTemplates.com

Charting Your Financial Course/ C. Grant Conness and Andrew M. Costa. —
1st ed.
ISBN 9798557707268

Contents

*To dedicated family, team members, and wonderful clients who have
helped us grow Global Wealth Management into a leader among
independent fiduciaries offering financial retirement planning
in South Florida.*

When you take income from your portfolio,

controlling volatility is key.

—C. GRANT CONNESS

—ANDREW M. COSTA

MANAGING DIRECTORS AND CO-FOUNDERS

GLOBAL WEALTH MANAGEMENT

Preface
C. Grant Conness

You're listening to a favorite song on the radio. You start singing along, feeling good about life, and then . . . an overzealous disc jockey interrupts the ending, or the channel cuts away early to an obnoxious commercial.

An abrupt halt to a favorite tune can leave behind a sour note.

For me, however, it was my business sense as much as it was my musical ear that signaled the end of my previous career. I had a sudden realization it was time to kill the music and embark on a new path.

I quit playing bass for a promising band on tour, a daring move I felt was necessary to begin building a new life altogether, but the decision created its share of turmoil I had to overcome.

****

In sixth grade, I bonded with some Fort Lauderdale friends through a budding fascination with music. Like many hopeful musicians in their first bands, a garage was the ideal backdrop to begin practicing guitar riffs neighbors probably hoped would subside over time.

When we reached high school, much to the neighbors' dismay, the band's popularity actually surged. I remember one night feeling battered and bruised after playing in a physically demanding football game before one of our scheduled gigs. I played on the line for a perennial Florida prep powerhouse,

Cardinal Gibbons Catholic High School. I wondered if it was worth the trouble of joining the band for a show at a local club after the game, but I was stunned when I dragged myself there and saw about 500 kids lining the parking lot waiting for the doors to open.

The crowds, the vibe, and the excitement the group generated with our rock/reggae mix exhilarated me, but they did not distract me from a goal I promised my parents—a college degree.

Football, for me, played into that objective. Florida, a hotbed for high school recruiting, was a good place for me to showcase my ability. I attracted interest from a legendary coach who was building a strong program in the Midwest. Being a bit undersized as a lineman, I was projected as an NCAA Division II player. Eventually, I accepted a scholarship offer from the University of Findlay, a private university with an enrollment of approximately 3,000 in Findlay, Ohio.

The man who coached the Oilers, Dick Strahm, happened to own a vacation home in Naples, Florida, which enabled him to develop contacts with Florida high school coaches. Over the years, Coach Strahm established a fertile pipeline with prospects from Cardinal Gibbons.

Through those contacts, he recruited me. I played as both an offensive and defensive lineman for Findlay. I contributed on both sides of the line and also played on special teams during the 1997 season when our team soared to a 14-0 record. The season culminated in a national championship for Findlay.

It was a first for me, being outside of Florida for an extended amount of time. Living in the Midwest, I learned about the people there—good people. That experience, the people I met, and my education all became an invaluable part of my life. There were no shortcuts or excuses in that environment, being in a smaller school rather than a larger school. I also realized being an undersized lineman left some aches and bruises that took time to heal. Ohio winters had a harsh bitterness about them, which I could do without as a Florida native, especially since my heart was still set on playing in a band.

I flew home when I was still up at Findlay to play bass guitar for a weekend down in the Florida Keys. We played on some houseboat about a mile offshore for some crazy sandbar thing. I thought, "Oh my God, this is really what I want to be doing."

Students were on break after that championship season, and I returned home. It was then that I made the difficult decision to leave Findlay and quit playing football. I called Coach Strahm and informed the coach I was grateful for the opportunity to compete for a national title, but I wanted to be closer to home. I enrolled at Florida Atlantic University, in Boca Raton, where I earned a bachelor's degree in business administration.

I joyously reunited with our band, Carnegie Tide. A warm stage proved much more pleasant than frozen tundra. Another musical set played on the beach in a T-shirt and shorts was more agreeable than another quarter played on the gridiron in helmet and pads.

Connections provided opportunities, and, after I graduated from college, the band played concerts as a leadoff act for KC and the Sunshine Band, as well as other national touring groups. Carnegie Tide played on both coasts and at large venues across the country.

Unfortunately, I learned promises are often left unfulfilled in the music industry. Promoters tout opportunities to make it big. That chance to catch a big break, however, rarely pans out.

I was twenty-seven and dating my future wife, Jessica, when we had a heart-to-heart about where things were headed. The band wasn't cutting it, our future was at stake, and we decided a fresh start was necessary.

I had grown to like Southern California and relocated there. There I could pursue another passion, surfing, and possibly work for a surf wear manufacturer.

Then I had another idea, which now seems obvious. Why not pursue a career associated with my college degree?

There was one problem. I had no business contacts in Southern California. I posted my resume online and received a request to interview with an independent financial advisor, but the vibe just wasn't right. Frankly, the advisor came off as condescending—a valuable lesson, it turned out, because I vowed then and there to treat clients in a respectful, personable manner.

Another opportunity arose . . . oddly enough, in the same office building, only with a different financial advisor.

The moment I walked into that office, I sensed I could make a favorable impression. The décor featured just about anything that could be stitched, stamped, or stenciled with logos of the Tampa Bay Buccaneers. I almost felt like I was back in Florida where the Bucs captivated the whole state during their 2002 NFL season with a victorious Super Bowl run.

Although this financial advisory firm was manned by just one advisor and an office assistant, we forged a warm relationship right away.

I became involved in real estate and was successful. But, a tipping point soon became evident when Jessica and I, after saving for a down payment on a house, began looking at available real estate in Southern California. We were ready to take the plunge for homeownership, but the exorbitant price on the starter home caused us to reconsider.

Instead, we thought it might be time to return home. I placed a call to Florida, reaching out to Andrew Costa. I was acquainted with Andrew through friendships that linked our two families. We also attended the same schools growing up in Fort Lauderdale.

It so happened that the real estate ventures I was doing in California were beginning to gain popularity in South Florida. We reconnected, though Andrew worked in insurance at the time, and I eventually started my own Florida firm specializing in real estate investments.

The desire to build my own practice was driven by the gains that could be made in real estate in the mid-2000s. Then, the Great Recession hit in 2008. Just about anyone involved in real estate was battered by the financial crisis. I was no different.

For me, the most vivid memory of the downturn was an opportunity to accompany Kirra, my oldest daughter, to a campout. What should have been a special night to be with my daughter began with an agonizing call I made to my father. I needed to borrow 200 bucks to pay for the registration.

I was frustrated and embarrassed. I wondered where my life was headed and what my dad, who was always there for me and graciously provided the money needed for the campout, was thinking about his son needing a paltry 200 bucks. I wondered what Jessica was thinking back home, with two other kids in diapers and a fourth child on the way.

But, I have always been driven. Even when I didn't have enough money to take Kirra to a campout, she still enjoyed it because, well, what kid doesn't like eating gooey hot S'mores with her dad?

That was where I decided, "I'm going to figure this out and make sure this isn't how I'm going to live my life." Ever since then, I've worked hard, started this business, and made sure I could provide for my family.

The business I launched alongside Andrew in 2009 is Global Wealth Management. Our practice has become one of the fastest-growing independent financial planning firms in South Florida. Ever since we opened our doors, I have been playing a different tune—one that has been on-key and uninterrupted.

Preface
Andrew M. Costa

The first vivid memory for me regarding some sort of financial peril happened during a long car ride. I spent six hours riding home to Fort Lauderdale during a semester break from Florida State University.

I didn't think much about what the ride would entail. Just another trip home for some time with family, away from undergraduate studies and the campus scene I was beginning to enjoy. Not long, however, after I got in the car and was headed out of Tallahassee, I sensed something was dreadfully wrong.

The driver was clearly overwrought. Clearly distracted. Clearly hiding something.

The man behind the wheel was my father.

****

At the beginning of the new millennium, after surviving the overblown Y2K scare about what havoc the imaginary bug could wreak on the world's computer programs, many investors began appropriating funds into the dot-com boom.

Online shopping and communication companies became overvalued, contributing to what became known as the dot-com crash, which stretched from March 2000 to October 2002. Many of the companies affected were significantly tied to information technology that expanded exponentially when computers became more common—and more necessary—among American households.

At the time, I was essentially still a kid who had gone off to college. I was not entirely aware of my father's financial position, and I was completely unaware of my father's investments.

But, when I got in the car that day to go home, thinking it would be an uneventful ride from Tallahassee to Fort Lauderdale, the conversation did not pivot to a typical father-son chat about school. In fact, when I attempted conversation, my dad only grimaced and mumbled.

I could just kind of read it in his face, and I kept asking him, "What's the deal? What's going on?" He just really didn't want to talk about it. I could tell it was more than just him having a bad day, so I kept trying. After all, something had to give over the course of a six-hour drive spanning pretty much the whole state of Florida.

Dad finally broke down, which was strange because he was really as tough as you can get about most things. He just said, "Son, your mother and I have lost about everything we saved for retirement in the bubble crash."

Various emotions gripped me all at once, in part because I did not yet have a complete grasp of how such a financial setback could occur.

I was sympathetic to my parents and their plight. However, a different emotion was the most powerful of all. I was angered by how this could have happened, and I couldn't fathom the effect it could have on our family's future.

Reconciling with this anger was difficult at first. I was uncertain how someone with a strong knowledge of investment principles could suffer such a devastating loss. How could no one have anticipated the dangers of the dot-com bubble? Based on my own general understanding, it seemed as if my father had run with a pack of investors who were unaware of the inflated value of those stocks.

But, I could not voice any resentment. These were my parents. They had made a commitment to provide me the funds for a college education. I knew they would continue to make financial sacrifices to help me earn an undergraduate degree in finance from Florida State.

I thought for the first time in my life, "Wow, I really need to get serious here. I need to be there for them." That day was a growing-up moment for me. Later, I learned it's not so easy when you are the one actually experiencing the financial woes.

Surprisingly enough, though, things worked out rather smoothly after I entered the financial industry.

I befriended an older businessman who ran a couple of large companies. We would enjoy lunches together, and I would soak in any business advice the gentleman wanted to dispense. One day he mentioned a niche area of the market regarding premium-financed life insurance. The older acquaintance indicated he was thinking about a venture into this line of insurance and thought I would be a good fit, too.

The prospect excited me, even though I didn't know much about the product. That motivated me to immediately learn every nuance regarding premium-financed life insurance. I did my homework and learned this type of insurance involves borrowing money from a third-party lender.

While the loan must be paid back with interest, funds inside the life insurance policy grow tax-free and can potentially be used to cover the costs of the loan. This type of policy is often purchased by those with high net worth and was especially popular during the timeframe in which I started as a licensed insurance agent.

Eventually, however, interest rates and market factors changed the game. I was again left to re-invent myself. I reconnected with

Grant, as he mentioned, and together we began discussing potential business opportunities.

After catching up a little on life, I learned Grant's situation was dire following the losses he incurred from the Great Recession. I was not undergoing the same financial strife, but I grew increasingly concerned about economic factors.

I asked myself, "If I don't figure something out here soon, then what do I do?"

Although Grant had expended his savings, I knew how much my friend was driven to succeed and support his family. Grant was in a tough place, but he was as hungry as anyone could be to figure things out. I had some of the financial wherewithal to help plant the seed, and together we started a financial advisory business.

We knew in our hearts we were going to make things work at Global Wealth Management. Both of us had mentors who influenced us toward becoming traditional financial professionals.

For me, the troubles I saw my family go through also left a lasting impression. It motivated me to get my own finances in order.

Grant and I realized we had a passion for doing things the right way, with a little bit more of a conservative approach than others.

We wanted to protect the savings people have worked hard to accumulate. To do this, we wanted to put together financial retirement plans for people to follow versus just sort of having an investment that doesn't have a vision to it. Together, we have made this vision a reality for Global Wealth Management so our clients don't have to experience a long, uncomfortable car ride like my dad and I did.

CHAPTER 1

This is Your Retirement, Questions Must be Asked

"Life without a defined purpose is similar to a boat without a crew in the middle of the ocean."

–Anonymous

Global Wealth Management stemmed from many inspirations and motivations, perhaps none more than the financial situation facing Andrew's parents, which he learned during that unsettling ride home from college.

Following that ordeal, which we detailed in the preface, Andrew learned about financial advisors who were engaged in what seemed like unscrupulous practices. He learned how risky investments could exhaust someone's retirement savings far too quickly, and he also learned of precautions investors can take to avoid such pitfalls.

His frustration with his parents' situation led to a bedrock certainty on which Global Wealth Management was established: Clients should ask however many questions it takes to be satisfied and should never feel discouraged by their advisors. Being involved in the process of building, managing, and preserving your assets is a necessary part of prudent investing and should be encouraged and aided by an advisor who keeps your interests at the forefront. This is *your* money. Money you worked diligently to save. It's quite likely a percentage of those funds, quite possibly a large chunk, were constructed from saving a portion of each paycheck you earned and setting aside a regular allocation into a 401(k) account or other retirement savings plan. Because this is your money, you are entitled to have dedicated help from those whose services you enlist.

Time to Take an Additional Step

After all these years of building a retirement portfolio, why would you avoid a financial advisor who can adequately craft a plan for your retirement?

Having overcome the lean times—times when you questioned saving for retirement in order to meet other expenses—you have a considerable reserve to show for the discipline you exerted. Now it is a question of preserving that nest egg throughout the period of life we call retirement.

Now is the time to enlist a trusted professional who can help you address any concerns you have about your savings or any mysteries you need help unraveling. Perhaps you feel a bit puzzled about how to plan for income, investments, taxes, legacy, or health care (what we reference as the five pillars of retirement).

Asking questions and testing the mettle of any advice you receive is a crucial part of the process, as we learned from one of our seminar attendees.

A distinguished professor, Mr. Phipps, attended one of the financial seminars we host at various locations in South Florida. Mr. Phipps had recently retired from his tenured position at a college in New York. He moved here to enjoy the Florida warmth— which is, of course, quite common.

Believe us when we say most potential clients have questions. If they attended a seminar and then follow up with an office visit, they're engaged in both their own personal situation and the process we use to construct a thorough plan.

Mr. Phipps happened to pose a provocative question.

"In order to choose the right person to manage my retirement funds, what should I be asking?"

Have you ever watched a televised interview and seen a public figure—say, a politician, a coach, or an entertainer—react as if a question was truly intriguing? Maybe the question was phrased in a way the subject did not expect. Maybe it touched on something the person had never been asked before. Questions like those often elicit a genuine response.

In the case of Mr. Phipps, his question changed our approach to financial planning. After he spoke, we got to thinking about our business model.

Mr. Phipps made us think of questions clients should be asking, which essentially struck at the heart of what we do as advisors. Thinking of the client first, and the questions they *should* be asking, helped to broaden the level of trust we are capable of building with aspiring retirees.

Obviously, people do not always know to ask these questions. Nonetheless, we try to mention the following issues while listening intently to people's retirement ambitions and life stories.

Four Questions to Ask When Choosing a Financial Advisor

1. As my advisor, will you ask me questions?

Retirement planning can seem complicated, and it probably is confusing to someone with little background in finance. You should ask questions when making the important decision of selecting a financial advisor. After all, the advisor and his or her firm is working for you, not the other way around.

Nonetheless, the process does not work if the client is the only one who is inquisitive. In fact, the advisor should also know what questions to ask and how to proceed with any concerns.

To generate a plan for retirement, the advisor must get to know the clients well enough to understand their hopes and ambitions. This is the only way the advisor can be prepared to incorporate the proper methods for facilitating clients' retirement visions.

No matter how detailed you might be in terms of what you want to achieve in retirement, the advisor must drill down and obtain specific information in order to prepare a plan that best suits your needs with the funds you have available.

It's important to ensure your financial advisor has a complete picture of your financial situation *and* your goals and aspirations because, if one piece of your financial outlook is out of whack, everything else could be thrown off as well. To illustrate, think of foot pain painful enough to seek medical attention. A foot functions with a complex mechanical system consisting of multiple bones, joints, muscles, tendons, and ligaments. If something within that structure is strained, it can cause great pain. Walking—a basic part of many of our lives—becomes a painful exercise. A client who was a competitive tennis player once told us, "When your feet hurt, your whole body hurts."

The same can be true if a portion of your retirement portfolio is not performing properly within the network of financial mechanisms diversification is designed to create. Hearing from clients about how they want those funds to work on their behalf, based on retirement goals, is a fundamental appraisal any financial advisor must make.

Initial questions pertaining to home ownership, personal debt, health considerations, and the presence of a will or trust are relatively simple. But they direct the advisor down a logical path to help show the client many elements needed within a comprehensive retirement plan.

From there, an advisor will ask more detailed questions. The first should concentrate on the rate of return you desire for your investments. This question helps determine our clients' aversion to risk. Different approaches can be constructed based on different levels of risk. If a client's heart rate spikes at the mention of a 10 percent loss, that person's plan will differ from someone who is unfazed by the possibility of losing 15 to 20 percent of their stock portfolio in a market downturn.

Personal questions, of course, provide specific rationale behind risk allowance. For example, does your income currently meet your monthly expenses? Do health factors threaten, or already cut into, your income? At what levels, if any, do you support children or grandchildren? Could you be put into a position in which you help fund any health-related expenses for a parent or loved one?

Questions regarding the death of a spouse are also important and are a key reason for couples to be together when they attend sessions we conduct. Often, one person in a marriage handles the vast majority of financial considerations, whether it's paying the bills or handling investments. Regardless of who takes the lead in family finances, it's important for both spouses to have a basic knowledge of both the short-term financial factors, such as budgeting, and the long-term ones, such as investment strategies.

It is imperative to examine consequences that will play out upon the passing of a loved one. In addition to the emotional impact stemming from the death of a spouse, the financial impact can have significant consequences, too.

A couple who had moved to Florida from New Jersey visited us and was aware of a significant income gap that would arise if the husband died. He received a pension payment, which totaled about $80,000 annually. He was in his early seventies and about ten years older than his wife, so there was a strong possibility he would pass away first. If he did, however, the entire pension would be lost. In addition, a significant portion of the couple's overall Social Security distribution would also disappear. The fallout from such an event would leave the wife with about $30,000 annually, exclusively through Social Security.

The husband's state pension included a single-life benefit, in which monthly payments are based solely on the lifetime of the person receiving the pension and stop upon that person's death.[1] To counteract that, the couple had about $250,000 in retirement savings, which was not being touched as they received income from both the pension and Social Security. We suggested a future income stream from these savings could help offset the substantial gap that would arise annually for the wife if the husband preceded her in death.

In the end, this couple did not incorporate the plan we suggested. Why, we couldn't say. They didn't tell us. We suspect it was because we could not devise a model that would provide the wife with the same annual income the couple was receiving through the funds provided by the pension. The couple did not become our clients that day, and we wished them a long, prosperous life.

Legacy questions are also pertinent to retirement planning, even in the early phases.

A dear lady, Francine, visited with us about some choices she was considering after being retired for several years. When we got into some basic questions about her lifestyle and how that could

---

[1] Many pensions include a joint and survivor benefit, which determines payments based on the lifetimes of each spouse. The surviving spouse still receives benefits following the death of the other spouse. Unfortunately, this option was not the case for the couple because they had already made a permanent decision on the pension payout options long before we met.

be facilitated, we quickly recognized she was quite frugal. In all likelihood, she would never need to touch her portfolio of investments totaling almost one million dollars.

When we asked about her heirs, however, Francine noted she wanted the flexibility to always have funds available in case her children needed her assistance. Without knowing that specific desire, Francine's funds may have been wrapped into investments that would not have provided the liquidity she required to help her children, if necessary.

Different avenues exist for building legacy arrangements, and knowing a person or couple's considerations and priorities sooner rather than later is key in building a plan that specifically works for them.

2. What kind of plan will work for me?

This is an open-ended question, considering no two retirement plans are alike. Nonetheless, the question should at least prompt the advisor to think about the specific details needed to construct a personal plan based on information obtained from you. This goes back to why the advisor should be asking you several questions, particularly at the outset of any relationship you build.

What an advisor should convey is, for them, each workday involves creating, or modifying, retirement plans. These plans differ in many ways based on resources investors have built, ambitions for retirement years, and intentions for what clients want to leave their loved ones. Other factors, such as risk aversion, debt elimination, and long-term care protection, also must be incorporated into a plan.

A blueprint must be constructed for how to handle expenses when your days accumulating wealth through a steady income stream have ceased. A well-crafted plan enables a retiree to realize goals *and* adhere to a fixed budget. Also, retirees often assemble various retirement accounts containing different amounts of money, but a process is needed to combine everything within a set plan designed to capitalize on all those assets. This process also holds the advisor accountable once a retiree has implemented the plan.

An independent fiduciary will not be tied to a specific company and will not sell you a specific line of investment products. The fiduciary standard of care involves acting always in the client's best interests, even if doing so runs contrary to the advisor's own interests. The Securities and Exchange Commission, which regulates registered investment advisors as fiduciaries, stipulates the fiduciary:

- Act with undivided loyalty and utmost faith.
- Provide full and fair disclosure of all material facts, defined as those which a reasonable investor would consider important.[2]

Your advisor should be intent on preparing a diversified retirement plan for you to follow. That plan should be built to account for a long life, especially since aging continues to trend upward with more medical advancements and better awareness of exercise and nutrition.[3]

3. How often will we meet to review my plan?

A financial advisor who checks in with you only when the market is doing well might not have your best interest at heart. Getting to the heart of the issue, though, is not altogether difficult.

---

[2] Coryanne Hicks. U.S. News & World Report. March 21, 2018. "What Is a Fiduciary Financial Advisor?" https://money.usnews.com/investing/investing-101/articles/what-is-a-fiduciary-financial-advisor-a-guide-to-the-fiduciary-duty

[3] USC Leonard Davis School of Gerontology. Infographics. 2018. "Americans Are Living Longer." https://gerontology.usc.edu/resources/infographics/americans-are-living-longer/

Clients often enjoy conversations we create through periodic and personalized reviews of their retirement plan. Yet, there is no need to wait for a scheduled meeting to ask an advisor a question. Just call. Questions pertaining to a prescribed plan are only natural.

Life happens. Customizing a plan means creating flexibility to accommodate changes. The sooner an advisor is aware of a situation that could affect your finances and your lifestyle, the easier it is to adjust your "Retirement Roadmap."

One more thing about the initial meeting: Make sure to personally visit the advisor's office and inspect the level of activity. The viability of the business can often be measured, in part, by the appearance of the office. Obviously, some variations are inherent with different practices. Still, the presence of full-time staff can be an indication of whether or not a firm has a significant amount of assets under management.

If an advisor is calling on you and wants to arrange a consultation at your home, I'd think twice. An office visit should enable you to confirm the advisor does not work out of his or her vehicle—a sign, perhaps, of an inexperienced practice.

Understand, too, that cold calls are not normal and could be an indication the business is struggling.

4. What is your fee structure?

Independent fiduciaries, such as the financial retirement advisors at Global Wealth Management, have considerable flexibility in their roles.

A fee-only advisor can remove middlemen involved in the investment process to potentially save you money on your investments. They do not accept fees or commissions based on specific product sales, and operate without an inherent conflict of interest. If you are someone who likes to be hands on, trade your own portfolio, or who has time to manage investments, a fee-only advisor can be your sounding board for decisions. It can be like going once a year for a tune-up on your vehicle. This is typically a flat, upfront fee.

Many people don't have the time, expertise, or interest to manage their investments day-by-day. They want to make sure a team of skilled individuals can manage within the confines of their risk tolerance and investment objectives in order to make sound decisions with them. This type of advisor is a fee-based advisor. This is typically an ongoing asset-based fee, although some fee-only advisors will occasionally earn commissions from product sales as well, which they should disclose to you.

We believe you will want to choose an advisor who does not solely earn commissions or trading fees and is compensated independently of the investments recommended. An individual who solely earns money through commissions is often not a true advisor and is instead considered a broker or insurance agent. They are typically incentivized to sell the next best thing that comes their way. This type of relationship tends to be transactional.

Frankly, you should not have to ask your advisor how they are paid. They should volunteer this information as a good faith act of transparency. By acting as fiduciaries, their obligation is to prioritize the interest of their clients first and foremost and be forthright with how they are being compensated. Either the advisors will be paid commissions off what they sell you, or they will charge fees for their services (though some administer both charges). We usually suggest you choose the advisor who does not earn commissions or trading fees and is compensated apart from the investments they recommend.[4]

Such advisors provide services paid for directly by clients and do not receive additional compensation, such as payments from fund providers. By acting as fiduciaries, their obligation is to prioritize the interest of their clients first and foremost.

5. Who holds my money?

You are likely only one of several clients your advisor serves. That advisor cannot be expected to manage the funds, and all the different variables that entails, for each client. The inefficiency of such an approach would be stifling. Imagine if the market takes a turn. Who does the advisor choose to serve first?

We believe an advisor should work with an institutional management team that oversees funds. That team enables the advisor to focus on building the right plan for you to follow, and amend, when you are approaching or are in retirement.

A related, important question can be stated quite simply: "Where is my money being held?"

The advisor should be aligned with a reputable custodian and not transferring your funds into their personal or corporate bank account. Common custodians are usually firms like Charles Schwab, Fidelity, or TD Ameritrade.

The investment scandal involving Bernie Madoff, and the elaborate Ponzi scheme he was found to have concocted, is a good primer for what can go wrong with trusting an advisor to handle funds directly. Know the custodian your advisor uses. Also, make sure any checks you write go directly to an investment fund or

---

[4] Coryanne Hicks. U.S. News and World Report. March 21, 2018. "What is a Fiduciary Financial Advisor?" https://money.usnews.com/investing/investing-101/articles/what-is-a-fiduciary-financial-advisor-a-guide-to-the-fiduciary-duty

custodian. Our custodian for Global Wealth Management is Fidelity.

CHAPTER 2

Ten Years to Retirement: Now What?

"Being the first to cross the finish line makes you a winner in only one phase of life. It's what you do after you cross the line that really counts."

–Ralph Boston

What amounts to the first lap for those heading toward retirement should not be a time for retirees to recognize they lack financial aptitude. Unfortunately, in America, even the most rudimentary courses designed to help with financial literacy are often not taught in our schools.

This is not only true for grades K-12 but also in college. Unless you major in business or finance, it is possible to complete a degree without securing any credit hours in personal finance. This dearth of financial knowledge permeates numerous professions.

It is not a huge stretch to link this problem to the credit card debt some young professionals accrue, even after they obtain jobs with nice salaries, following college graduation. A study by the National Financial Educators Council found, of more than 2,500 respondents of diverse ages, races, and educations, lack of knowledge about personal finances cost an average of $1,279 per person in the last year.[5]

Other findings revealed 44 percent of Americans cannot cover a $400 emergency with cash, 43 percent of student loan borrowers are not making payments, 38 percent of American households have credit card debt, and 33 percent of American adults have saved no money for retirement.[6]

Keep these statistics in mind when a co-worker shares a stock tip or a family member volunteers to help with your investments. While they mean no harm, much of the time friends and family who want to bend your ear about finances or even attempt to "make the numbers work for you" possess little expertise. What's more, even the most experienced financial advisors can disagree on tactics for wealth accumulation, preservation, and distribution. Financial mechanisms can be complicated.

One absolute, however, is the one person dependent on your financial success can be found in your mirror. It's you. Anything you can do to enhance your financial knowledge is a sound idea at any point in life, particularly when you sense you are nearing retirement. In fact, anything you can do to help yourself feel assured about retirement, as opposed to feeling hopeful—or worse, pessimistic—is worthwhile.

---

[5] PRNewswire. January 8, 2020. "Deficits in Financial Literacy Cost Americans a Lot of Money, Study Shows." https://www.prnewswire.com/news-releases/deficits-in-financial-literacy-cost-americans-a-lot-of-money-in-2019-survey-shows-300983018.html

[6] Dani Pascarella. Forbes. April 3, 2018. "4 Stats That Reveal How Badly America Is Failing At Financial Literacy." https://www.forbes.com/sites/danipascarella/2018/04/03/4-stats-that-reveal-how-badly-america-is-failing-at-financial-literacy/#5d544a4c2bb7

Phases of Your Financial Livelihood

Three separate periods define your existence as it relates to finances. The beginning of the sequence corresponds with the first time taxes are removed from your paycheck. FICA taxes are usually as prominent as anything levied on your paycheck. These payroll taxes are based on percentages from earnings paid to employees.

FICA stands for the Federal Insurance Contributions Act, which was approved in the 1930s as part of the "New Deal" program introduced by President Franklin D. Roosevelt. FICA taxes have two components. Social Security (OASDI) was enacted in the 1930s. Medicare was added as part of "Great Society" legislation enacted under President Lyndon B. Johnson.

For 2020, the FICA tax rates for employees were 6.2 percent for Social Security and 1.45 percent for Medicare. Employers match those percentages for a total FICA contribution of 15.3 percent. Those who are self-employed pay the entire FICA tax on their own and can do so on a quarterly basis using an instructive worksheet the IRS provides for Form 1040-ES.[7]

THE ACCUMULATION PHASE

When a Social Security number was attached to your identity, this was your introduction to saving for retirement. You started doing this without anyone, in all likelihood, informing you of the details behind the federal programs pinching at your paycheck in order to create some kind of safety net for you later in life. This was probably, even if you didn't realize it, your introduction to the first phase of financial livelihood.

---

[7] Amanda Dixon. Smartasset. "All About the FICA Tax." Oct. 24, 2018. https://smartasset.com/taxes/all-about-the-fica-tax

To become eligible for Social Security, you need to work at least ten years. The Social Security Administration uses a system of credits to determine eligibility. Four credits are essentially earned for each year worked, and forty credits are needed to qualify for Social Security.[8]

Recall one of the aforementioned statistics: 33 percent of Americans have no retirement savings. For many of those people, Social Security might be the only source of income they will be able to tap into during retirement. In a sense, this is money that was saved, except the government dictated taxes be taken from their earnings rather than them saving it themselves. The worker had no recourse but to accept the withdrawal imposed.

Today, the efforts of each individual vary greatly in terms of their individual savings, though the inability of some Americans to save for retirement could trigger an economic crisis. That threshold may not be difficult to reach in a period when baby boomers compose the bulk of new retirees, meaning 8,000 to 10,000 Americans are turning sixty-five every day.

Obviously, the more these people augment their expected level of mailbox money (Social Security, company and/or state pension) by saving into 401(k) programs or IRAs, the better off they will be when tapping into the savings needed to facilitate their lifestyles in retirement.

The process of compiling these future income sources is all part of the accumulation phase, which typically is the longest of the three financial phases of life. This is when you long for retirement, without completely knowing what retirement may bring.

But, it's not as hard as you may think. Savings add up, often quite fast as interest compounds. Also, it can be surprisingly easy

---

[8] Social Security Administration. 2020. "How You Earn Credits." https://www.ssa.gov/pubs/EN-05-10072.pdf

to not ever miss the money you contribute to a company 401(k), which sometimes includes a percentage the employer pitches in for a matching fund. The key is to just get started. Even if an employer does not offer any kind of retirement program, let alone a company match, savings can build over time if wisely invested. The accumulation phase requires discipline, and there are plenty of temptations to quit making those regular contributions. But, remember, the key is to not give up.

Keep the lifestyle you want to enjoy in retirement in mind, and realize the average U.S. life expectancy (as of the writing of this book) is 78.93 years.[9] Americans should recognize they could live well beyond the retirement date they observe, which means they will likely need more money for that retirement.

To simplify matters, ask yourself how many people you've known who lived into their nineties. Leading a long, prosperous life is an admirable goal and should alert people to the need for adequate savings. You can never save too much.

THE PRESERVATION PHASE

Reducing exposure to risk is a key element in retirement and requires diligence to make sure all facets of your portfolio reflect your goals. Your retirement savings represents the discipline you exerted to build various funds. You do not want that money to be reduced by an untimely market correction.

At this point in your life, in most cases, five to ten years out from retirement is when an appointment with financial retirement advisors can be quite helpful. A system that enables a fiduciary to examine risks in a portfolio and make suggestions regarding potential changes can help alert an aspiring retiree to

---

[9] Macrotrends. "U.S. Life Expectancy 1950-2020."
https://www.macrotrends.net/countries/USA/united-states/life-expectancy

potential risks possibly lurking within accounts they have worked hard to build.

In addition, it is important that the advisory firm can refer you to professionals who specialize in various aspects of planning, such as attorneys and accountants who can help with estate planning and tax preparedness. Global Wealth Management has advisors who can customize personalized retirement plans and put you in touch with qualified professionals for other needs.

THE DISTRIBUTION PHASE

That paycheck you were once accustomed to receiving during your working life will suddenly disappear when you retire. While you are no doubt aware that this is the way it goes when you're not working, the immediate impact can be somewhat startling.

This is your introduction to the distribution phase of your financial livelihood, where it could be necessary for you to begin making choices on funds you withdraw from your retirement savings.

While the preservation phase may necessitate hiring a professional to help assess how best to protect the assets you have accumulated, professional help could become much more important in the distribution phase to help you figure out how to generate income from your assets in a tax- and fee-efficient way that keeps more money in your pocket.

Starting with the B-Word

A wise exercise to try before entering retirement is to conduct an experimental dispersal of monthly expenditures designed to help you eventually cope with a fixed budget. Make sure everything is counted, including any round of golf, any movie (with popcorn), any yacht cruise, any occasional concert or play, or any meal at your favorite restaurant. Any activities that cost money must be accounted for to prepare an accurate ledger. Once the numbers are in, you may find a juicy ribeye might be just as tasty off your own grill as it is in the gourmet restaurant downtown.

Conversation between spouses can be a bit delicate when rating your favorite non-essential expenditures. You may hold on to a steadfast belief that neither of you can cook. Your lives were so busy while working you decided an alternative to cooking best suited your time constraints, so you never bothered with anything too daring in the kitchen.

In retirement, however, there's far more time to fill. Doing so in a way you find productive makes for a far more rewarding retirement. Developing new hobbies, or becoming hooked on old hobbies, is advisable.

Who knows? Gardening may become a passion. Golf may become something you not only tolerate but get reasonably good at playing. Crafting could become a way to decorate with your own flair and style. The more extensive list you create, the more possibilities you will have to keep you active, which is important while making concessions to adhere to your retirement budget.

With that in mind, it can be advantageous to divide retirement income into two categories: "paycheck" and "play-check." The first, of course, covers the cost of essential obligations. The second helps you enjoy an active lifestyle.

Add your mortgage, utilities, cable, phone, car, grocery, and credit card bills. Stopping there, however, will not provide an accurate assessment of expenses. Collect a year's worth of information. If you're not into filling out ledgers, so be it. Just count a year's worth of debits in your checking accounts. The number should be reflected on each of your monthly statements. Your bank might even provide an annual total. If not, the addition is simple. Be prepared for some sticker shock. The meals and coffee you regularly purchase, an annual membership of some sort, or a piece of furniture (it won't be the last you ever buy), adds up.

It can be advantageous to categorize obligations and expenses into the following categories:

- Necessary: food, housing, clothing, transportation, health care
- Annual requirements: property taxes, insurance premiums, auto registrations
- Somewhat essential: cable television, country club, gym, subscriptions, dues
- Non-essential: dining, entertainment, travel

Also, do not omit money you spend on your children. This can range from spotting them occasional cash all the way to paying for college or student loans. Among parents with adult children, 79 percent were found to provide some financial support for living expenses, both large and small. Plus, almost three out of four parents put their children's interests ahead of their own retirement needs.[10] Take time to reflect on this and ponder what your commitment to your adult children will be, both in terms of standard and emergency expenses.

Discovering every potential expense can help with future attempts to stretch your budget through prioritizing. Frugal decisions, especially if made while still accommodating the lifestyle you desire, are smart. No amount of savings is too much.

---

[10] Merrill Lynch Bank of America Corporation. "The Financial Journey of Modern Parenting." 2018. https://www.ml.com/the-financial-journey-of-modern-parenting.html

CHAPTER 3

Beat the Fear
and Learn the Concepts

"It is not the ship so much as the skillful sailing that assures the prosperous voyage."

–George William Curtis

Retaining the assistance of a financial advisor can be intimidating for some, sort of like re-living a fearful moment from their youth.

Like the time you got in line to ride the roller coaster and either braved the thrill ride or chickened out and exited the other way while others were boarding.

Or, the time you got into the batter's box and saw a pitcher's curve ball whizzing right at you before it tailed over the plate where you either stepped into your swing or bailed out.

Or, the time you dinged the car as a newly licensed teen and either told your parents about the light pole you struck or decided to keep it quiet. (For those who kept their mouths shut, your parents saw the dent anyway, didn't they?)

Following through on making a first appointment with a financial advisor seems to make some people fidget, almost as if they're a seventh-grader standing against a gymnasium wall attempting to get up the nerve to ask someone to dance.

Many of our clients came to us after previously seeing other advisors, and many were influenced by the pending transition to retirement and wanted a second opinion. The thing is, maybe the last advisor didn't turn out so well. Or, maybe they didn't communicate to you as well as you were hoping. Either way, knowing what advisors are talking about can help alleviate some of those cold feet.

So, let's start off with some basic concepts and processes we touch on during our initial discovery phases with clients. These are all elements we consistently revisit throughout all stages of the relationships we build with our clients, while realizing the financial retirement plans customized by the team at Global Wealth Management require regular updates. Some of the topics we touch on now will receive further examination later in the book.

Emergency Fund

A common problem we find among people who save for retirement is they get so focused on growing long-term accounts they have little in liquidity set aside as a rainy-day fund.

Tax advantages contained in funds intended for retirement income also carry penalties on withdrawals from such accounts before the age of fifty-nine-and-one-half. Income tax, as well as a 10 percent federal tax penalty, can be levied on such withdrawals, which also could incur fees an investment management company might charge.

This makes it imperative for savers to attempt to set aside an emergency fund to cover unexpected expenses. Never assume nothing unusual will arise. Medical bills, home repairs, insurance hikes, and kids' activities are all occurrences that can potentially deliver an unexpected sucker punch to the pocketbook.

One man, Pete, turned fifty and worried about the depressed industry he worked in. In spite of cutbacks both to the product line and the workforce, Pete was able to persevere and was even appointed to a management position created because of consolidation efforts. Not only was this positive, so, too, was Pete's ability to save money while stressing about job security.

All the funds Pete directed toward retirement (approximately $1.5 million) represented virtually all the money he had saved. Nothing was set aside in an emergency fund.

Unfortunately, his wife encountered medical issues, which resulted in some hefty bills. In addition, their daughter was involved in high-level dance competitions, which required money for instruction and travel. Also, the air conditioning at his home went kaput—never a good thing in South Florida.

Unfortunately, Pete didn't have a spare $20,000 or more lying around he could access easily. In order to pay various bills, they applied about $50,000 to credit cards, which carry exorbitant interest rates that made it difficult to pay down such debt.

Taking money out of Pete's IRA would incur the 10 percent tax penalty Uncle Sam imposes on those who make such withdrawals before fifty-nine-and-one-half. But, after some examination, he discovered the 401(k) plan he contributed to at work allowed him to borrow against that plan and not incur a penalty or tax liability as long as he paid the money back. Instead of boosting his account value, his contributions would pay off the loan within a relatively short amount of time. A bit of that money could also go toward building an emergency fund.

Although Pete and his family will have to find ways to pinch, they recognized the importance of saving money and were not altogether that extravagant in terms of lifestyle. Now, much more than before, they understand the importance of an emergency fund.

The need for an emergency fund is something we stress, especially to younger clients. Clients who are nearing retirement, or are in retirement, have often built emergency funds—sometimes they haven't, and provisions must be made to set aside some kind of reserve. The first time you withdraw funds for an emergency will not be the last.

Debt Elimination

Imagine we want to spend an ideal day boating but cannot get anywhere we want to go because the anchor gets snagged and cannot be raised.

Debt plays a similar role in weighing down our financial successes. Just like debt in other sectors of American life, whether it was created from government or consumer spending, retirement debt is an ever-increasing problem for the U.S. citizenry.

Tragically, this is even truer for the age group near retirement than for any other group. According to the Federal Reserve Bank of New York, "The total debt burden for Americans over age seventy increased 543 percent from 1999 to 2019."[11]

Debt in retirement, a time when people live on fixed incomes, is incredibly hard to eliminate and overcome. The average commercial bank interest rate on credit cards was a staggering 16.88 percent in November 2019.[12] Debt can cause people to live

---

[11] Greg Iacurci. CNBC. February 26, 2020. "Debt Among Oldest Americans Skyrockets 543% in Two Decades." https://www.cnbc.com/2020/02/26/debt-among-older-americans-increases-dramatically-in-past-two-decades.html

[12] Board of Governors of the Federal Reserve System (US), Commercial Bank Interest Rate on Credit Card Plans, Accounts Assessed Interest [TERMCBCCINTNS],

a substandard lifestyle, which can possibly lead to skimping on obligatory expenses such as quality food or medical care. Debt can be a burden that exhausts retirement savings far too quickly.

Downsizing

Downsizing a home can help retirees in many ways, though they may have to reconcile an emotional attachment to a long-term home.

One couple who became our clients moved into their neighborhood almost fifty years ago. Diana was an elementary teacher; Jim a state biologist. They bought a house in a friendly neighborhood where residents shared conversations along the fence lines, trick-or-treaters rarely skipped past a darkened porch, and the persistent thump of basketballs was heard on driveways.

Not long after adding a special touch to their "starter" house, a large Victorian home across the street struck Diana's fancy. As her family grew, she couldn't take her eye off the majestic property, which sat on a large corner lot. For whatever reason, there was little activity going on at the place, so one day Diana knocked on the door. An elderly lady answered, and it wasn't long before the two hit it off.

It so happened that Mrs. Poort had lived in her home for roughly a half-century. She had no immediate family. Other relatives lived out of town, and she received few visitors except for a niece, who was a nurse and checked in to make sure her aunt was getting along okay. Diana essentially became a close friend who engaged in conversation and, in the process, learned a great deal about her community.

---

retrieved from FRED, Federal Reserve Bank of St. Louis. Dec. 17, 2018. https://fred.stlouisfed.org/series/TERMCBCCINTNS

On those visits, Diana also took appraisal of the large Victorian dream home. While updates were in order, the house was structurally sound. When Mrs. Poort passed away suddenly from an illness, Diana and her family sold their home. Boxes, furniture and appliances were simply carried or wheeled across the street.

The home became a showcase. Diana gladly accepted her turn hosting meetings for both her civic group and book club. Jim's rec room was always a favorite for buddies to visit on poker night.

Over time, however, the rooms, the stairs, and the maintenance became more challenging. Diana managed, despite aching hips. Consideration was given to moving into a smaller home with only one level. The couple stayed, though revisions and repairs continued to unfold.

Just when all their projects were completed, Jim died.

Obviously that kind of jolt can be something that expedites a decision to leave a large home and downsize while in retirement. Yet, the sense of community Diana felt now included the presence of grandchildren. Grandma's big Victorian house on the corner still teemed with activity among kids ranging in age from kindergarten to high school.

Hip replacement surgery eased some of the pain Diana felt climbing steps. Accommodations were made to convert a spot downstairs into a bedroom. All the activity was something Diana decided was emotionally comforting for her, a sound reason to remain in her large home.

Others, however, overcome any sentimentality to stay put and find downsizing actually frees them of responsibilities that weigh them down in retirement. The question to ask is, "Which is right for me?"

Diversification/Risk Aversion

The longer investors can ride a bull market, the more they begin to feel impervious to the adverse effects of a downturn. Budding confidence can make them feel as if they command Wall Street.

Let's say your portfolio is worth $380,000. A whole lot of people would not want to even risk 10 percent of that amount, especially if the date you hope to retire is drawing close. Yet, if a downturn results from a market crash similar to 2008, the corresponding loss to a $380,000 portfolio would be about $150,000. That represents a 40 percent reduction.

Every investor is different. However, based on our experiences assessing risk aversion, most would be willing to lock in a return.

What if the number you lock in allows for no more than a 15 percent loss? Your portfolio would fall to about $323,000. Still, that's a much better outcome than a 40 percent loss.

These are the types of questions and scenarios we ask to determine a risk level for each client using a number between one and one hundred. If you happen to be a thirty-three, for instance, you would be thrilled with, say, a 9 percent bump in your portfolio but also would accept a 5 percent loss.

Different investments, particularly in disparate products—stocks, bonds, cash, annuities—can allow for growth in your portfolio despite losses incurred in one investment. Diversification within a specific investment can be vital, too, rather than, say, maintaining one individual stock holding.

Inflation

Inflation can eat away at the purchasing power of your money over time.

In the years leading up to the publication of this book, inflation was exceedingly low. From 2012 to 2019, the highest rate was 2.3 percent in 2019.[13] Counting on low rates of inflation, however, would mean ignoring long-term historical trends.

Protecting against inflation is an important consideration in retirement. Investments such as stocks and mutual funds have the potential to keep pace with inflation. Treasury inflation-protected securities (TIPS), real estate securities, and commodities are other possibilities. Social Security benefits are automatically indexed to inflation.

Regardless of the specific tools and strategies you intend to use for retirement, taking into account how they work together to account for these factors is critical.

---

[13] Kimberly Amadeo. the balance. Jan. 29, 2020. "US Inflation Rate by Year from 1929 to 2020. How Bad Is Inflation? Past, Present, Future." https://www.thebalance.com/u-s-inflation-rate-history-by-year-and-forecast-3306093

CHAPTER 4

Global Wealth Women

"The more you know who you are, and what you want, the less you let things upset you."

–Stephanie Perkins

As women generally outlive their husbands, it should come as no surprise that most women will eventually find themselves exclusively in charge of household finances. Studies show, currently, 40 percent of women are the heads of their households. Among them, 37 percent out-earn their partners and 63 percent are single mothers.[14]

It's indisputable: Financial savvy is an important facet of life for women, both now and in their futures.

Yet, the financial industry is lagging behind. Only 17 percent of all financial advisors are women, according to data compiled by Investment News.[15]

---

[14] refinery29.com. Jan. 17, 2018. "What The Modern American Family Looks Like – By The Numbers." https://www.refinery29.com/en-us/women-breadwinners-household-income-family-impact?bucketed=true

[15] Joni Youngwirth. Investment News. Aug. 8, 2018. "The rise of the female financial adviser."

This lack of representation can have adverse effects for women when it comes to financial planning. One example: Statistically, women outlive men. In a husband and wife pairing, the wife will typically outlive her spouse by many years—years in which she will have to plan for the loss of the lower Social Security check, possibly the loss of a pension, and the hit of being pushed into a higher single-payer tax bracket. Unfortunately, in our experience, many couples come into our office with plans that fail to address these circumstances and the myriad other issues that come with women's extended lifespans.

Now, in many couples, we find there is often a financial alpha and a financial beta—someone who takes the lead in the areas of finance, and someone who tends to be removed from the financial decision-making. Many studies show the alpha may be most involved in investing, while the financial beta may take the lead in day-to-day financial decision-making and the family budget. Many studies show, while previous generations saw men acting as the financial alpha, for the boomers and beyond, men and women may exchange or share roles when it comes to their finances.

Nonetheless, the financial industry has been slow to react to such trends, indicating women are taking additional control of household finances. No matter what the financial dynamics of a relationship—who does the budgeting, and who does the investing—during the first phase of our retirement roadmap review, we stress the need for both partners to understand the significance of the process.

We understand financial planning is not something everyone enjoys. If necessary, we will meet on an individual basis with those involved in a relationship and touch on all five pillars of

---

https://www.investmentnews.com/article/20180808/BLOG09/180809930/the-rise-of-the-female-financial-adviser

retirement planning—income, investments, taxes, health care, and legacy arrangements. Nonetheless, the construction of a couple's retirement plan is based on factors that affect each partner. Each needs to gain an understanding of the components to be better prepared in the event a partner passes away.

No matter what your family dynamic looks like, we want you to consider: What would your spouse do if you weren't here? Who will inherit your portfolio? How will your spouse manage things without you? Who can they turn to?

That's a gap we want to help fill as an independent fiduciary firm. We strive to make a surviving spouse comfortable in his or her own ability to follow and understand a comprehensive retirement plan.

This is a particularly relevant discussion for women because, while everyday expenses are managed by a whopping 85 percent of women in this country, only 23 percent orchestrate long-term financial planning.[16]

That isn't to say women can't be successful in long-term finance. In fact, we could argue just the opposite. In the book, *Smart Women Finish Rich*, American financial author David Bach cites how an analysis compiled by Fidelity Investments revealed women generated investment returns at half a percent higher than men.[17]

The U.S. Census Bureau, in fact, reports approximately 80 percent of married women outlive their husbands. Often, those

---

[16] Susan John. U.S. News & World Report. May 8, 2019. "Why Women Should Handle Financial Planning." https://money.usnews.com/money/blogs/the-smarter-mutual-fund-investor/articles/why-women-should-handle-financial-planning

[17] David Bach. davidbach.com. Copyright 2018. *Smart Women Finish Rich ®: 8 Steps To Achieving Financial Security And Funding Your Dreams.* https://davidbach.com/wp-content/uploads/2018/09/Smart-Women-Finish-Rich.pdf

very women wish they would have been more active in financial matters when their husbands were alive.[18]

This is just one of the many reasons to develop a lasting relationship with a financial advisor. We assure clients that, at Global Wealth Management, we are committed to growing our business and to interacting attentively with everyone affected by the retirement plans we prepare.

The Creation of the GWM Women's Division

In growing our firm, one of our greatest achievements has been the creation and ongoing development of Global Wealth Women.

Amber Kelly, the director of Global Wealth Women, came to the company as someone who has spent years providing counsel to financial advisors around the country. She has helped build suitable and ethical practices while working directly with all types of financial firms. As a licensed Investment Adviser Representative, Amber works with our clients to develop comprehensive financial plans encompassing issues such as income planning, retirement planning, asset protection strategies, investment planning, and estate planning.

Amber is dedicated to empathizing with women who may be recently widowed or divorced. She relates the complexities of retirement planning with compassion, expertise, and professionalism. Women on the GWM staff also work with men and couples while providing fresh perspectives. We believe this is something invaluable to how retirement plans are constructed by Global Wealth Management.

---

[18] Jean Chatzky. The Balance. "How Women Can Plan for Outliving Their Husbands." Oct. 1, 2018. https://www.thebalance.com/retirement-plan-for-women-outliving-husbands-4139845

We realize, too, that women encounter different needs. Those needs reference the statistics we just mentioned regarding longevity. Women may also be affected by the demands, and stress, created by the nurturing desire to be a caregiver to parents or children. Additionally, they may experience more potential hardships that stem from not being part of the workforce for a period of time, such as for a leave of absence for childcare. These factors can all affect earnings and, thus, retirement savings.

Meanwhile, women with varied backgrounds who experience various household circumstances continue to attend our seminars, inquire through our website, and visit our offices every day.

Dynamics shared by women who have visited Global Wealth Management include, but are not limited to:

- A single mom who finds herself reviewing different investment strategies while also attempting to plan for her children's futures. She is currently battling with the alarming expense of college education.

- A widow whose husband dealt with financial matters she never worried about. When her husband passed away, she was left to fret over the financial portfolios. The strategies her husband implemented were devised without her input.

- A divorcee who is left to cope with financial concerns created in part by the separation from a spouse and a new living arrangement.

- Someone who is considering a divorce and wants the confidence to know they are going to do the right thing financially.

- A partner in a healthy marriage who hasn't previously been involved in the long-term financial decision-making of their household.

Building on Alpha Instincts

So, to what lengths can the financial alpha be stretched?

Well, each partner in a relationship could be involved in finances. Based on couples who consult with our team at Global Wealth Management, we find more partners who are each actively involved in finances. This is an indicator the traditional roles often embraced by baby boomers are changing.

In addition, we also see partners in second marriages or in new relationships. Quite often, each establishes a financial foothold that identifies assets belonging to each spouse. Quite possibly, each has their own fervent beliefs about finances.

We also confront situations where divorcees could be hoodwinked by investment managers working at big-box brokerage firms.

Tracey, a fifty-eight-year-old divorcee and small business owner, scheduled an appointment with Global Wealth Management and shared concerns about an advisor she began seeing after her divorce. Tracey's age obviously pegs her as someone who is nearing retirement. As such, it was quite conceivable Tracey could find it advantageous to reduce risk in a portfolio that was heavily committed to the market.

Her advisor (by trade)/salesman (by nature) continually tried to assure Tracey she was too young to have a financial plan crafted for her to follow in retirement. To her, it almost seemed as if her investment advisor was trying to flatter her into thinking she looked young, and, therefore, she was young when it came to retirement considerations.

Quite frankly, the opposite is true. We believe it's never too early to begin preparing for retirement, though there comes a time when it can be too late to build an adequate retirement portfolio—

especially if one's only savings are socked away during what they hope are their final years in the workforce.

Tracey's business had already given her a deep appreciation for some of the more difficult conversations surrounding retirement. She provided services helping others place loved ones into care facilities. Her business helped people plan for their futures. Unsurprisingly, that's what Tracey essentially wanted out of her advisor. What was even more puzzling, and egregious, was that Tracey actually wanted to retire and her advisor was apparently not listening. Tracey wanted her advisor to do more than just nod his head yes without examining her portfolio thoroughly to determine if retirement was feasible.

"I don't want him just to tell me it's okay," Tracey told us. "I want proof. I want knowledge. I want to see it, and you know what? I'm not too young. I want to sell my business. I want to retire. I'm sick of hearing that my financial advisor is just going to take care of me. I want to do it on my own. I want that understanding from an advisor who can help with a plan."

Again, this is what makes a customized, written plan so comforting. Our process, which we call the "Retirement Roadmap Review," is prepared through a series of steps—only after both the client and the staff at Global Wealth Management agree a workable fit can be achieved by both parties.

The strength Tracey showed in recognizing her advisor was not working in her best interests was commendable. Her story was also proof women are often thrust into situations where they must become actively involved in some, if not all, decisions involved with retirement planning. We also hope to show other advisors they should listen to their female clients rather than assume they have no interest in or concern with their finances.

Our Services Are Designed for You to *Live*, Not Fret

Financial planning "stuff," as some people call it with a dismissive tone, isn't as fun as a day at the beach, a seat at a grandchild's ballgame, a cruise to the Caribbean, or a short boat ride to Bimini. We get that. It's why we do what we do, attempting to simplify the process by performing various functions designed to stretch your retirement savings and require less work from you.

And, it's why people like you seek the services of financial advisors in the first place.

Think of the top professional athletes. They constantly seek the advice of a highly skilled set of instructors. As an example, stroll past the driving range prior to a competitive round at a PGA or LPGA event. To the naked eye, each golfer is striping the ball accurately at intended targets with a swing that looks divine. Yet, coaches can detect the slightest flaws and offer input designed to generate the best results.

The process used on the practice range underscores an important point we can relate to retirement planning: Not everything can run on autopilot. As short as the water ride is to Bimini, the boat will not float there on its own. This is a point we stress to both men and women.

Janis and Her 'Advisor'

Janis (a name we'll assign to one of our clients) had gone through a divorce, and, after dealing with the stressful legal procedures, she realized she was financially on her own. She consulted with an investment advisor who, during a three-year uptick in the market, was able to generate good results in growing her portfolio. To be truthful, it was a period when any worthwhile advisor should have succeeded with investments, and Janis' advisor did no less.

While Janis was genuinely happy to have made gains in the market while going through some emotional turmoil, she sensed a volcano bubbling. Volatility in the market was looming overhead, and the conversations with her advisor continually centered on opportunities for growth.

Concerns regarding his approach prompted Janis to arrange an appointment elsewhere. During a consultation with Amber, our director of Global Wealth Women, Janis shared thoughts about her investment advisor.

Janis wasn't completely distrustful of him. In fact, she remained appreciative. "Mark really helped me through a dark time," Janis said. "I had been married for twenty-two years. There were times I was an emotional wreck, even though I knew the divorce was the right thing for both me and my ex. When you're moving on from a marriage, though, stocks, bonds, index funds, and all the rest . . . it's not something you care to think about. Frankly, I never thought about it much to begin with."

Janis had been influenced by one of the first television ads she saw promoting a big-box firm she had heard of previously. She didn't know it based on the ads, but it was a firm intent on essentially forcing its advisors—brokers, actually—to peddle company products they earned commissions from selling, based on the amount of money invested into the product.

While she found "Mark" to be somewhat pushy at times, an allegiance developed because of the vulnerability Janis felt as a recent divorcee. Plus, Mark's abilities, in the end, did generate gains in her investments. When she told us of this relationship and the conflict she was feeling about a change in advisors, we told Janis we were not in the business of breaking relationships.

We did, however, tell her about the fiduciary standard we must uphold, under law. We defined the characteristics of wealth accumulation, which Mark was likely encouraged to augment under a suitability standard. Then we informed Janis of the preservation and distribution phases of wealth management and how they fit into her vision as she approached retirement.

She felt she was at a point, after moving past her mid-fifties, where it made sense to adopt a more conservative approach. Yet, she was fearful of initiating a breakup with "Mark" and worried about any objections that might spark. She had noticed, however, during the three-year period with Mark, that she heard from him less and less. Also, he had never offered to construct a financial plan for Janis' retirement.

This was a case where Janis was grateful for an opportunity to speak to a female advisor. Gently, Janis was instructed to thank Mark for his time and his assistance before telling him, "I'm at a different point in my life, and I've decided to move in a different direction."

We want to emphasize one point through this story. With any investments an advisor suggests, the relationships and the insights are truly meaningful. But, in the end, this is *your* money. When someone tells us, "I don't want money to ruin a relationship with my current advisor," the comment can be heart-wrenching because of how much money is under consideration and how important that money is to someone's successful retirement. This is what the prospective client worked so hard to earn. This is their retirement that is potentially being subjected to risk. This is their livelihood. This is high stakes. So, go ahead. End it. It's your money, and it's worth more than a business relationship.

As people approach retirement, they need a plan based on their needs and their vision. At Global Wealth Management, our express purpose is to build such plans.

No Boarding Restrictions for Women

We love when women get on board with a retirement plan whether they are married or in a relationship. If single, divorced, or widowed, we realize it can be even more imperative they commit to a plan.

The U.S. Census Department collects census data every ten years. The 2010 census revealed a disproportionate number of men sixty-five and older were married (72 percent) compared to women (42 percent) in the same age group. In addition, a higher percentage of women were widowed (40 percent) compared with widowers among men (13 percent).

These numbers carry great significance for women, considering the 2010 census found 40.3 million Americans were sixty-five or older. That segment composed 13 percent of the U.S. population and represented a massive leap from 4.1 percent in 1990.[19]

The senior set has continued to grow. Additional statistics also support the premise that women should be willingly involved in household finances, including retirement savings and the use of those funds in retirement.

Trust, however, is an issue. In our interactions at Global Wealth Management, we can sense women are more comfortable speaking with other women about financial matters.

Again, this is why we created Global Wealth Women, a division devoted to financial services designed specifically for women. Amber continually examines approaches GWM uses during

---

[19] Richard Eisenberg. Forbes/Next Avenue Contributor Group. July 1, 2014. "Who are Americans 65 and Older?"
https://www.forbes.com/sites/nextavenue/2014/07/01/who-are-americans-65-and-older/#9f1c893fdb48

individual Retirement Roadmap Reviews while working with all our clients.

Often, we discover women are savvy investors who exercise more caution than men. This is a strong trait, since conservatism can help extend a retirement portfolio. It's something we stress to all our clients.

****

Sometimes, women are more comfortable working with a male advisor, perhaps because of some connotation suggesting he is a stronger educator. In many cases, though, women are relieved to speak to a female advisor about finances. The female advisor can sometimes be more relatable and less intimidating, and thus establish greater rapport and trust.

Look, we all know circumstances in life change in a heartbeat. Global Wealth Women can provide a platform in which women can come together, in a safe space, and ask any question.

Often we've found, too, that men prefer working with a female advisor, especially those who recognize, if they pass on before their spouse, they want a female advisor to consult with their wife.

We are continually building Global Wealth Women because we believe both men and women are equally able to handle their retirement finances, as long as they have adequate counseling. We pride ourselves in being at the forefront of issues, like the topic of women and money, with a platform that accommodates everyone.

CHAPTER 5

Retirement Roadmap Review

"Age is an issue of mind over matter. If you don't mind, it doesn't matter."

–Mark Twain

So, how long will you be retired?

This is the quintessential question with no answer. No one can predict how long they will live.

Factors can be applied to the equation, ranging from your quality of health to hereditary markers. Still, you just never know. A reasonable assumption, particularly if you have not yet retired nor set a retirement date, is your retirement will last roughly a quarter-century.

Statistically, people are living longer, though the effects of drug overdoses, obesity, and diseases have been attributed to leveling off some life expectancy predictors.[20]

Some can remember grandparents or possibly great-grandparents who planned for a retirement that lasted around

---

[20] Thomas R. Frieden. The Washington Post. Jan. 11, 2018. "U.S. life expectancy is dropping. Here's how to fix it." https://www.washingtonpost.com/opinions/us-life-expectancy-is-dropping-heres-how-to-fix-it/2018/01/11/c6aa6420-f3b4-11e7-beb6-c8d48830c54d_story.html?noredirect=on&utm_term=.1a45381bbae1

fifteen to twenty years. Today, longevity dictates it is wise for people to plan for a retirement that could last up to forty years and possibly outlast the time you spent working.

Not only does that encompass a long period of time, it also requires a detailed plan to be followed stringently to make sure your income lasts as long as you do.

Yet, with retirement planning, many wait far too long to piece together their investments and consult a financial advisor qualified to prepare a plan.

Today, the funds you have saved must provide more coverage in case you live long in retirement. Circumstances vary, but, when we prepare an initial plan, we often build it out with the assumption clients will live to be ninety. That is, frankly, a generous estimate. The potential, however, for a life lived into a person's nineties demands we build conservative plans intended to make portfolios last.

Not too long ago, retirees relied on pensions and conservative investments that carried much higher interest rates. Retirement planning was simple enough that, for many people, a specialist was not needed to help with income planning and making sure investments could cover someone throughout the length of their retirement.

Today, company pensions have largely vanished, and interest rates on simple investments have been curtailed. Creativity in retirement planning has become much more essential.

Our process at Global Wealth Management is called the "Retirement Roadmap Review."

It begins when prospective clients fill out a confidential, ten-page financial questionnaire during what we call the "Discovery Meeting."

We ask about interests, hobbies, concerns, goals, values, relationships, previous advisors, assets, and investment processes.

We also ask, what would constitute the ideal vacation? These elements compose the total client profile.

From there, we ask a multitude of questions in order to craft an income plan, health care plan, legacy/estate plan, and investment plan, including:

INCOME

- Is your current cash flow sufficient and comfortable?
- Do you have a strategic plan for taking your required minimum distributions from IRAs?
- Do you anticipate any significant changes in cash flow?
- What are your projected Social Security and/or pension benefits?

HEALTH CARE

- Do you have long-term care?
- How is your health?
- Are you using Medicare or Medicare Advantage?

LEGACY/ESTATE

- Do you have any life insurance?
- To the best of your knowledge, are your accounts titled properly and with up-to-date beneficiaries?
- Are there any other estate planning concerns you want to address?

INVESTMENTS

- Do you understand your underlying investments?
- Are you familiar with how your investments are working together on behalf of your plan?
- Do you think your allocations reflect your risk tolerance?

TAXES

- Are there any upcoming life events that may change your taxes?
- Are you currently receiving tax refunds?
- Do you know your current effective tax rate?
- Have you had a Roth conversion tax analysis prepared?
- Are you looking for strategies to minimize your taxes in the future?

All this information is processed after the initial Discovery Meeting, where your current plans related to income, investments, taxes, health care, and legacy are reviewed. It's okay if these elements have not been incorporated into formal plans for you yet. Quite often, we will get stacks of statements related to each of the five pillars of retirement rather than sophisticated, formal plans.

****

Making your money last long enough is imperative to a fulfilling retirement.

Think about someone in your life who retired before you even considered the prospect. Maybe think back to when you were a kid and you spent a weekend at the home of your grandparents or great-grandparents. You knew they didn't work. But you had no clue how they generated an income stream, or that the process may have been simplified by the availability of mailbox money—say, a pension and Social Security. They also may have relied on a simple investment, drawing good interest at a local bank.

We want to again assert an important point: Today's retirement considerations can be complicated. To help understand the dynamics, think of what was available to your grandparents or great-grandparents, and what influenced their lifestyles in retirement.

They may have watched free television with a signal boosted by an antenna. They may have spent a good portion of their time reading a daily newspaper delivered to their driveway in the morning . . . and evening. They may not have considered traveling much at all if family was located nearby and grandkids' activities were at the local gym or ball diamonds. They used their phones—tethered, mind you, to a landline—only for conversation.

Today, we pay for the television signal we receive via a cable, dish, or internet service. Newspaper, periodicals, and books can be accessed online, along with numerous other sources of information, some of which are shielded by paywalls requiring online subscriptions. Kids' activities are sometimes far away, if they are skilled enough to play on traveling teams or attend camps.

> *"I fear the day that technology will surpass our*
> *human interaction. The world will have a*
> *generation of idiots."*
> *–Albert Einstein*

And then there's the smartphone—a personal possession many of us either carry or have at our side twenty-four hours a day. Consider some of the items a smartphone has replaced or mimics—books, calendars, contact directories, cameras, calculators, portable music, video players, camcorders, voice recorders, GPS, flashlight, portable gaming devices, barcode scanners, clocks, watches, alarms, timers, notepads, and laptops.

The smartphone is also a source from which we can exercise purchasing power.

Think about it. How many times do you use your cellphone to discover product choices, make payments, and process shipping?

How many of those purchases were instinctive, and, be truthful now, a bit irrational?

Those Chia Pets seemed so cute at the time, right?

Consider, then, the potential impact of the smartphone, as well as other technological advancements, in retirement. Discipline will be needed to reject impulses that prompt needless purchases.

****

Don't take this the wrong way. We are not averse to technological advancements. In fact, they assist us greatly because they have been incorporated into many of the analytical processes we use to evaluate variables within clients' portfolios.

When we begin to build a plan for someone, we're reminded of times traveling with our parents and riding in the back seat of the car on a summer vacation. This was long before devices existed in cars to calculate the shortest route to any destination.

Invariably, we would get lost at some point. We laugh, remembering our dads pulling the car over, unfolding a large map, and looking for the right place and the right road, sometimes after having to scramble to find a pair of magnified reading glasses.

Finally, we would get re-routed, and tensions would ease. Still, a half-hour was wasted attempting to get back on track.

Now, the devices we have in our car tell us if we have veered off track—"recalculating" has become a snide addition to our lexicon—and, in a couple of minutes, re-direct us down the right road. We're constantly updated on how long it will take to reach our destination.

This is relatable to what some people do in retirement. They get off track, and suddenly they're not receiving the right amount of income, or they've been pinched too heavily by taxes, or they lost an excessive amount of money in the market.

A viable income plan in retirement, however, allows you to zoom out, look at the big picture, and evaluate variables that could become factors over the next twenty, or even thirty, years. Market corrections, factors related to taxes, and income sources that can be tapped become clearer with proper planning. Aspects that could become problematic can also be identified and mitigated.

The retirement plan we prepare is designed to be navigated quite easily and doesn't even have to be folded just right, unlike that big map your father crumpled in a huff.

Let's move on to specifics we address during the three phases of our Retirement Roadmap Review.

RETIREMENT ROADMAP REVIEW

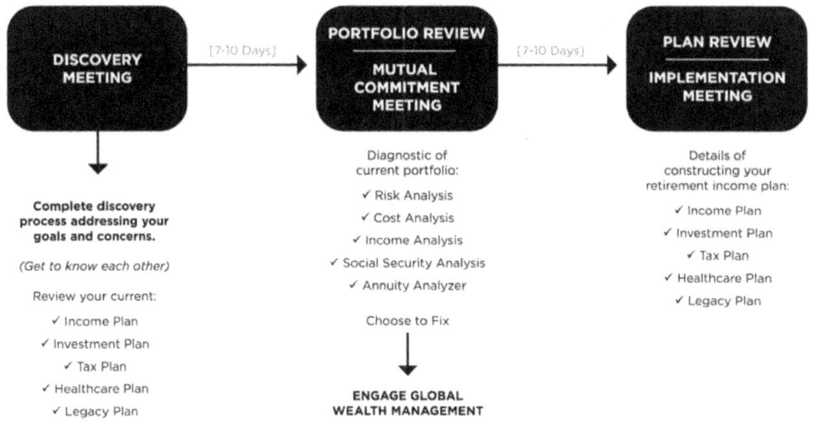

DISCOVERY MEETING

We ask numerous questions during the Discovery Meeting to help us get to know potential clients personally.

This is our chance to listen intently to the hopes and ambitions of those who have already retired or aspire to retire and want advice for how to navigate that transition.

We want clients to recognize the importance of preserving wealth from the very outset of our Retirement Roadmap Review. The plans we prepare apply a conservative approach while recognizing that Americans are living longer and the prospect of more medical advancements and better nutrition could continue to boost longevity.

We touch on the five pillars of retirement to provide an initial review of your current:

- Income plan
- Investment plan
- Tax plan
- Health care plan
- Legacy plan

PORTFOLIO REVIEW/MUTUAL COMMITMENT MEETING

After the initial Discovery Meeting, we conduct a Portfolio Review, which essentially runs a diagnostic of your current portfolio. We submit all components of the existing plan—or, if someone doesn't really have a plan, we at least submit the various parts of what they have—to a stress test. Analytics include:

- Risk analysis
- Cost analysis

- Income analysis
- Social Security analysis
- Annuity analysis
- Tax analysis

This is much like going into your doctor for a checkup. They check your blood pressure and pulse and sometimes order a blood panel to determine organ functions. These readings are necessary before a physician can make any medical recommendations.

The analytics we perform are similar. We need to determine what the diagnostics are before making recommendations.

This is a comprehensive process designed to identify any particular concerns while also building on whatever strengths the portfolio has. Sometimes the information can be rather startling, particularly in regard to the level of risk and the amount of costs tucked inside the investments of a potential client.

Yes, *potential* clients.

Not until we finish the second phase of the Roadmap Review with a thorough analysis of the portfolio will we look to build a mutual agreement between Global Wealth Management and a client, cementing our relationship.

Obviously, we want clients to be fully satisfied with the analysis we provide. In addition, if potential clients do not seem willing to follow the advice we provide as professionals, a relationship is probably not a good fit. We, too, reserve the right not to accept someone as clients.

Our top priority is for you to understand the conservative approach to planning we advocate. We stress a major point: in retirement, controlling volatility is more important than gaining the best returns on investments. Slow and steady wins the race, and typically it better protects the assets you want working for you throughout your retirement. We will address this phase much further in Chapter 8.

PLAN REVIEW/IMPLEMENTATION MEETING

After reaching a mutual commitment, usually within a period of seven to ten days, we schedule two additional meetings within the next thirty to forty-five days.

The first meeting dives into the details needed to construct a comprehensive retirement plan, and includes:

- Income plan
- Investment plan
- Advanced planning (often involving an attorney or tax advisor), which includes:
  - Tax plan
  - Health care plan
  - Legacy plan

We then schedule another meeting that serves as the onboarding process for the client experience at Global Wealth.

During this final meeting of the Retirement Roadmap Review, we address the following matters:

- Reiterate the structure of the plan
- Review accounts
- Review initial statements and website
- Establish a regular review process
- Implement advanced planning

More to Retirement than Just a Number

A television commercial a big-box firm once aired focused on a financial amount—a number—people attained for their retirement. It played into a general understanding people have about wealth accumulation.

That number only scratches the surface, however. Once that number is attained, it becomes imperative to understand what it can provide you. People begin to ask, "I've accumulated this money, I've worked all these years, now what? How is this total of what I accumulated going to generate income?"

You have crossed the bridge from the accumulation phase into the capital preservation and distribution phases. A plan for making your money last while generating the income needed to provide for your lifestyle in retirement is essential.

People become trained to look at returns and focus on appreciable gains that grow their accounts.

At the beginning of the Retirement Roadmap Review, one thing we stress to potential clients is that the goal is no longer centered entirely on fortuitous returns. Instead, the process we implement attempts to incorporate a sensible and prudent plan.

We can, of course, always make alterations to the plan. In fact, flexibility is advantageous.

Quite often, retirees recognize the opportunities they may have to enjoy traveling are best achieved early in retirement when their health is good and their energy level is high. Sometimes the concessions we build into a plan for such activities are a bit incongruous with the conservative approach we recommend, but we understand traveling is often a desire people want to achieve early in retirement.

We tend to insist, however, that plans be revised and followed according to those adaptations, so clients can travel where they want to in retirement and then scale back on expenses as they age. Others do not need that level of flexibility built into their plans, though plans should be reviewed frequently and amended if necessary.

An important point to stress: retirement planning will often have many complexities, but the roadmap we prepare is designed to ease any trepidation created by all the different variables.

CHAPTER 6

Gaining a Grasp on Social Security

"Should any political party attempt to abolish Social Security, unemployment insurance, and eliminate labor laws and farm programs, you would not hear of that party again in our political history."

–Dwight D. Eisenhower

I magine dining at a buffet and eating off plates embossed with the Social Security logo. Or, maybe something a little more personal—a stamped reproduction of your Social Security card. You know, the document so vital to your financial privacy, everyone advocates you keep it hidden under lock and key.

When you see the familiar Social Security symbol, thoughts probably race through your mind. Many of us think we know at least a little something about this popular government program, which was introduced in 1935 as a social insurance initiative consisting of retirement, disability, and survivors' benefits.

Considerations for timing the acceptance of benefits contribute to the imaginary buffet line. Although we pay a certain amount into the Social Security pool through payroll taxes, the benefits we are eligible to receive—much like items in the buffet line—are not equal. Those who wait until the maximum age of seventy to take benefits will get to dine on the prime cut of their Social Security allotment, while those who choose to begin receiving benefits at the age of sixty-two could be settling for cold cuts.

In spite of the substantial difference in the benefit amounts between the ages of sixty-two and seventy, deciding when to take Social Security remains, to borrow from the buffet options, a meaty decision.

The size of one's monthly benefit check increases from the ages of sixty-two to seventy, including an 8-percent addition for each year aspiring retirees wait beyond their full retirement age. Many people, however, cannot afford to wait until they're seventy, based on levels of savings and additional factors that influence how long they want to remain working.

Frankly, anyone who confidently boasts they can provide an accurate assessment of your Social Security considerations without examining your entire portfolio and learning your retirement aspirations is doing you a disservice.

The totality of an aspiring retiree's financial position must be understood when considering Social Security options.

Granted, you will want to make some calculations that include tax considerations based on provisional income, which is a measure the Internal Revenue Service uses to determine whether Social Security recipients are required to pay taxes on their benefits. But Social Security—much like life—is not just a math problem.

Timing for When to Begin Taking Your Social Security Benefit

For some, few decisions regarding retirement will be as instrumental as when to begin taking a Social Security benefit.

Often, those who feel pressure to get this decision right either have little retirement savings or realize a Social Security benefit could best augment what savings they do have, if taken at the most opportune time.

We use software that can help determine the best time to claim a Social Security benefit, though it is important to repeat the adage we stipulated earlier: *Life isn't a math problem.*

Sure, we can pinpoint any potential tax burden created by Social Security when a benefit is added to your income stream. From that, we can attempt to minimize the tax burden based on when a benefit is taken, while realizing the benefit is going to grow if you can wait to take the benefit at full retirement age. Or, better yet, wait until you turn seventy.

While any potential tax burden plays into the decision on when to begin taking Social Security benefits, other considerations also exist. Quality of life remains first and foremost among those.

Some simply sense an urgency to retire and express such desires during our Retirement Roadmap Review. That's perfectly fine. If this is a client's wish, we are happy to help them find a way by spelling out alternatives based on the different Social Security thresholds available to them. The Social Security Administration can capably answer questions regarding benefits available to aspiring retirees and answer questions about additional Social Security benefits. Social Security Administration employees, however, are not licensed financial retirement advisors and should not be relied upon for financial advice, especially based on parameters specific to you.

Establishing a My Social Security account with the Social Security Administration enables those paying into the system to gain a solid estimate for how much Social Security income they can expect to receive. The account also provides a reflection of earnings, which you should check for accuracy.

****

For some, insight into Social Security is restricted to the three distinct ages when benefits are impacted. Social Security for retirement can start as early as sixty-two, between sixty-six and sixty-seven (depending on when you reach what the government has determined to be your full retirement age), or at age seventy, when you can receive the maximum payout available to you.[21]

Your Full Retirement Age

Year of Birth	Full Retirement Age
1937 or earlier	65
1938	65 and 2 months
1939	65 and 4 months
1940	65 and 6 months
1941	65 and 8 months
1942	65 and 10 months
1943—1954	66
1955	66 and 2 months
1956	66 and 4 months
1957	66 and 6 months
1958	66 and 8 months
1959	66 and 10 months
1960 or later	67

However, myriad ways exist for when to claim a Social Security benefit. Let's take a look at one hypothetical couple—John and Jane. They're five years away from retiring—which they will do at sixty-six when they reach full retirement age and plan to begin

---

[21] Social Security Administration. 2020. "Full Retirement Age." https://www.ssa.gov/planners/retire/retirechart.html

taking their Social Security benefits. This would net $2,500 per month for John and $1,200 per month for Jane.

John has $850,000 in a 401(k). In addition, the couple has a joint account of stocks and bonds worth about $350,000. Those are invested, using a balanced approach, with approximately 60 percent allocated to stocks and 40 percent to bonds.

What becomes most important for them (this applies to any retirement plan) is the monthly amount ($6,000 in the case of John and Jane) they want to generate in after-tax income to support the lifestyle they desire in retirement. If we run their setup scenario through our income planning software, a stress test of their portfolio and their projected expenses unfortunately indicates that, without changes, if each begins taking Social Security at their full retirement age (sixty-six), John and Jane might have about a 65 percent chance of their money lasting throughout their retirement.

But, let's see what happens if they do something a bit different with their Social Security. One alternative is Jane starts benefits as planned at age sixty-six with the $1,200 monthly amount. John, however, could postpone taking his Social Security benefits to age seventy (realize each year a benefit is delayed from full retirement age to seventy, the result is an 8 percent increase). Waiting until seventy bumps John's monthly payment closer to $3,300.

Based on our analysis, this move could increase the possibility of their money lasting through retirement to 79 percent. With an additional risk analysis, they might also scale back some of the risks in their portfolio, as well.

By reducing risk and optimizing Social Security variables, for someone in a situation similar to the hypothetical John and Jane's, they might be able to increase the probability of their savings lasting through retirement significantly!

You not only get just one shot at retirement but also only one chance at declaring for Social Security, so it's prudent to carefully analyze that decision.

Provisional Income Can Affect Tax Burden

A common misconception is income derived from Social Security is not taxable. This is not the case. Social Security benefits can be taxable based on calculations for annual income. Additional sources of income, such as withdrawals from tax-deferred retirement savings, a pension, or a part-time job, could quite conceivably force you to pay taxes on Social Security benefits.

Like we mentioned above, there is a measure used by the IRS to determine whether recipients must pay taxes on their Social Security benefits. This method is called provisional income. Such income is calculated by adding a recipient's adjustable gross income, tax-free interest, and 50 percent of Social Security benefits.

Depending on a person's provisional income, the IRS could levy income taxes on 50 or up to 85 percent of their Social Security benefit. For taxes filed for income earned in 2020, the following amounts were imposed:

- Single filers:
    - Combined income of $25,000 to $34,000 paid taxes on up to 50 percent of their Social Security benefits.
    - Combined income of more than $34,000 paid taxes on up to 85 percent of their Social Security benefits.
- Married couples filing jointly:
    - Combined income between $32,000 to $44,000 paid taxes on up to 50 percent of their Social Security benefits.
    - Combined income of more than $44,000 paid taxes on up to 85 percent of their Social Security benefits.

The prospect of taxes paid on provisional income is a big factor when you are deciding when to take Social Security.

If you're going to get heavily taxed on your Social Security and you can fulfill that income need in a different way, you might want to delay Social Security as long as possible. Not only are you getting a higher benefit because it's growing at 8 percent a year, but you're also delaying a tax you may be incurring for no real need or reason.

Calculating Spousal Benefits

Often, spousal benefits are beneficial for those who may have spent long stretches outside the workforce—someone who stayed at home to care for children or for a sick or elderly relative, for example. Such a commitment created a gap in that person's working history in which no taxes were paid into the Social Security program.

A spouse who worked throughout this period stands to make more in terms of a Social Security benefit. A spousal benefit can be up to 50 percent of the primary wage earner's benefit at full retirement age.

One important point to note: If you were born on or after January 2nd, 1954, you can only make the choice to withdraw your benefits one way, one time. So, when choosing to take a spousal benefit or use your own earnings history for Social Security, the choice you make will dictate the check you receive every month for the duration of your retirement.

For example, a spouse who elects to take a monthly benefit at age sixty-two will be subject to a 67.5 percent reduction as opposed to being able to collect 50 percent of a mate's benefit after reaching full retirement age. That can result in a substantial difference in benefits, though many factors must be considered in

Social Security elections. Circumstances could dictate it is not best to wait, in an effort to maximize a benefit at a later age.

DIVORCE

Those who have gone through a divorce also can claim a spousal benefit if four criteria are met:

- The marriage lasted ten years or more.
- The former spouse has been divorced for at least two years.
- The former spouse has not re-married.
- The former spouse qualifies to begin taking Social Security.

This benefit does not require the ex-spouse file to receive a Social Security benefit before a spousal benefit can be filed.[22]

To provide an example, we'll use the names Scott and Marcia. They were married for fifteen years before their divorce, which happened when he was thirty-six and she was forty. Marcia remarried. Scott did so, too, though his second marriage ended after a few years.

Scott volunteered in schools much of his life, and his personal monthly benefit for Social Security is close to zero. Marcia, an educational administrator, chose to defer retirement and not begin accepting benefits until she turns seventy. Scott, still, can begin taking a spousal benefit based on Marcia's work history as early as sixty-two. The maximum he can earn, which is 50 percent of Marcia's earned monthly benefit at her full retirement age, can be collected at Scott's full retirement age. No claim Scott makes

---

[22] Social Security Administration. 2020. "Retirement Planner: If You Are Divorced." https://www.ssa.gov/planners/retire/divspouse.html.

will affect the benefit Marcia receives when she begins taking Social Security.

WIDOWED SPOUSES

If a marriage ends in the death of a spouse, it is possible to claim a survivor's benefit as the widow or widower. You can begin taking income at the age of sixty and, unlike the spousal or divorced benefit, a full benefit can be collected.

However, benefit amounts increase at specific intervals, beginning at sixty-two, then full retirement age, and lastly at seventy. If a spouse began taking benefits before he or she died, the widow or widower cannot delay withdrawing survivor's benefits to get delayed credits. The Social Security Administration stipulates you can only receive as much from a survivor's benefit as what your deceased spouse might have received, had he or she lived. The surviving spouse receives the higher of the two benefits. For example, if the benefit for the surviving spouse is $1,500 per month and the benefit of the deceased spouse is $2,500, the surviving spouse would collect the higher benefit.[23]

Working While Collecting Social Security Benefits

For those who begin claiming Social Security before full retirement age, the federal government imposes annual limits on income before reducing benefits by one dollar for every two dollars earned over the limit.

In 2020, the annual limit on earned income was $18,240.

When opting to take benefits before you reach full retirement age, remember you will be collecting a reduced Social Security

---

[23] Bethany K. Laurence. NOLO. "Will I Get Penalized for Working While Collecting Social Security Retirement?" https://www.nolo.com/legal-encyclopedia/will-i-get-penalized-working-while-collecting-social-security-retirement.html

benefit and, by working, you will put yourself in jeopardy of paying back half of what you earn after you reach the government threshold.

Predicting the Status of Social Security

Some bleak predictions have been made regarding the future solvency of Social Security. The program could be in jeopardy and this will be an issue that continues to prompt debate in Congress as lawmakers examine possible measures to enact.

The rate of retirees among baby boomers leaves fewer Americans in the workforce to support those collecting benefits. In 2011, money paid in benefits exceeded money collected for the Social Security Trust Fund, marking the first time money was allotted from the federal government's general fund. That allotment meant the Social Security program contributed to the nation's budget deficit for the first time.[24]

This is merely our opinion, but it seems highly unlikely Social Security will be abolished. Changes could be made, and have been already, to reset full retirement ages. Also, reductions in benefits could be enacted as another cost-cutting measure.

Practically all American workers (90 percent) paid Social Security taxes in 2018.[25] That same year, approximately 67.5 million Americans received a Social Security benefit of some kind.[26]

[24] Kimberly Amadeo. The Balance. Feb. 4, 2019. "Social Security Trust Fund, Its History, Solvency, and How to Fix It." www.thebalance.com/social-security-trust-fund-history-solvency-how-to-fix-it-3305890

[25] Jean Murray. The Balance. March 5, 2019. "Overview of 'Trust Fund' Taxes." www.thebalancesmb.com/what-are-trust-fund-taxes-clearing-up-the-confusion-4173679

[26] Social Security Administration. February 2019. "Monthly Statistical Snapshot." https://www.ssa.gov/policy/docs/quickfacts/stat_snapshot/

If the program were to just go away, we believe a nationwide revolt could occur. Retirees have long relied on this "mailbox money" to a fault, especially if their retirement savings are largely tied to the Social Security benefit they will receive.

CHAPTER 7

Three Worlds of Money

"If we are strong and have faith in life and its richness of surprises, and hold the rudder steadily in our hands, I am sure we will sail into quiet and pleasant waters for our old age."

–Freya Stark

Sounds pretty daunting, doesn't it, "The Three Worlds of Money"? Yet, it is a principle designed to help clients understand the diversification within the vehicles they can invest in.

The illustration helps break down three characteristics essential to all investments:

1. Growth/Income
2. Liquidity
3. Protection

Investors want all those attributes, but no single product is a perfect ten for all three. To get adequate amounts of each characteristic, we must navigate the three worlds and determine a "sweet spot" for each client based on assessments we make while conducting the Retirement Roadmap Review. That review compares their sweet spot with how their allocations are currently spread out within the three worlds.

We attempt to identify investments and financial vehicles that fit into each world and provide examples so you recognize what provides liquidity, what provides protection, and what provides growth potential.

If, for example, a client is invested heavily into products that create considerable growth and income potential, then it is likely they are also assuming a higher level of risk.

The "sweet spot" will include investments that bridge the three worlds and provide the diversity clients desire based, in part, on their risk aversion. Our goal is to take advantage of all three worlds to generate a portfolio that provides the growth and income, protection, and liquidity appropriate in a plan designed to make retirement savings last a lifetime.

3 WORLDS OF MONEY

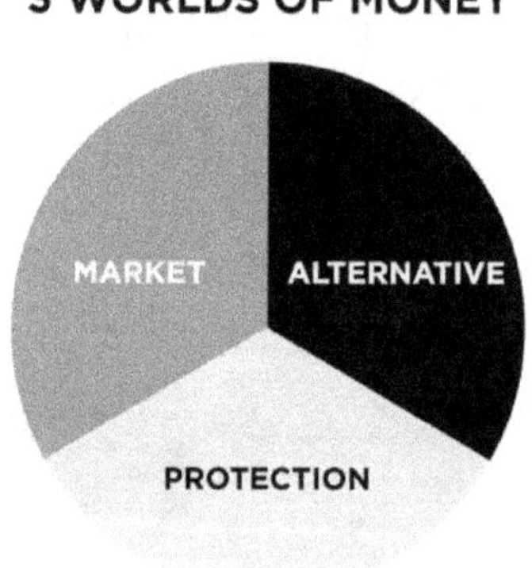

The three worlds are divided into these groups:

1. Market
2. Protection
3. Alternative

Let's explore each in greater detail.

MARKET WORLD

This world is usually correlated to growth and income. Quite often, we discover it is where most of our clients are heavily invested when they first consult with us. Sometimes investments in the growth category have a good deal of liquidity but very little protection. Stocks, for instance, offer no guarantees. The growth potential can be huge, but so, too, can a loss if a market correction occurs. Then, bam! You feel as if a contemptible pirate commandeered a chunk of your retirement pot and made off to sea with some of your valuables. You're left empty-handed, with no chance of getting anything back.

In retirement, you're no longer working, so you may not have the time or assets to wait for opportunities to regain money in the market. You really don't want to go back to work. Even ambitious retirees no longer have the time needed to rebound from steep losses incurred in a market correction.

Obviously, the allure of the market is great. We keep close tabs on our market allocations and hope to achieve nice returns in order to grow wealth. Yet, as we age, volatility associated with the markets makes such investments more perilous.

Investors, of course, are conditioned to seek solid returns. As you near retirement, however, that mindset should change. You should become focused on controlling volatility, a topic we address in the next chapter.

The following products do not contain much protection but offer the greatest opportunities for growth . . . and loss:

- Stocks
- Bonds
- Mutual funds
- Index funds

PROTECTION WORLD

This world happens to be the most tranquil, which means some might find it rather boring. Yet, as people approach retirement (a stage many clients are in when they arrange an initial consultation with us), the protection world becomes a potential haven for realizing retirement goals and making money last in retirement.

All that flash and sizzle investors became accustomed to as they watched stock market returns with the goal of building their portfolios must be tempered as retirement nears. Consistency and reliability become features aspiring retirees find welcome when they do not want their nest eggs threatened.

The following investments are backed by an insurance company (1), a bank (2), or a government entity (3):

- Life insurance (1)
- Annuities (1)
- Cash (2)
- Money market accounts (2)
- Certificates of deposit (2)
- Government-backed bonds (3)

ALTERNATIVE WORLD

This world consists of financial investments that are not correlated to stocks and bonds but also are not risk-proof. Such investments fall outside the realm of conventional investments such as stocks, bonds, and cash.

In addition, alternative investments often have low liquidity. An investor, for example, may own rental properties that have tenants. The lease agreement prohibits you from immediately selling the property, but, if the stock market dips, the house, building, or structure retains value.

The following investments do not have a large amount of liquidity and can be categorized as alternative investments:

- Real estate investment trusts
- Speculations
- Commodities
- Private equity/debt

******

We estimate 75 to 80 percent of the people we meet with about retirement are top-heavy in market allocations, subjecting their portfolios to considerable risk while attempting to grow accounts. That sends a troubling signal when little of the portfolio is dedicated to either the protection or alternative worlds.

Pardon the pun considering the subject matter, but this is not the end of the world.

As we previously stipulated, it's okay to be top-heavy in the market as you attempt to accumulate wealth. Typically, the market has the most potential upside of any investment. But, as you age, it becomes more imperative to diversify and make sure you are also allocated in the other worlds.

Let's say you're the person with all your investment money in your 401(k), and you're still working but at least beginning to consider the timing of your retirement. At the age of fifty-nine-and-one-half, most plans allow you to make an "in-service distribution" without a 10 percent early penalty tax on the amount being distributed. At this age, you can start to roll out money from your 401(k), which can then be invested in other vehicles.

Prior to reaching the age of fifty-nine-and-one-half, those who have the vast majority of their retirement savings socked into a

401(k) will find it difficult to make withdrawals without incurring substantial penalties.

One alternative in such cases is to begin decreasing contributions into the 401(k) between the ages of fifty to fifty-five. Savings can then be thrust into opportunities presented by the protection and alternative worlds. One issue to consider in this is to capitalize on funds an employer is willing to contribute to your 401(k) by matching your allocation.

Still, it is wise to at least build an emergency fund. The goal for such an account, which is completely liquid and can be accessed at any time, is for it to equal at least a half-year's salary. An unexpected major expenditure can be tremendously expensive if financed with a credit card.

****

What is important in retirement (or as you near retirement) is that the market still provides the greatest opportunity to build growth and income. In addition, the market can help combat inflation. Over time, your growth investments in the market could decline. Yet, even if you have only 20 percent of your portfolio invested in the market, with the other 80 percent invested in protective or alternative investments, that 20 percent in the market is important because it provides opportunity for growth and can help offset inflation.

Your "sweet spot" must still bridge all three worlds.

Timing a market correction is not easy. It really isn't worth trying. Most people get it wrong.

After the Great Recession and the economic decline it wrought in 2008, many people sensed periods in which they thought the market would again crash and panicked, at least to some extent. As they found out, missing out on a day when the market makes a big leap is costly.

Those people missed out on the prospect of appreciable growth in their market accounts because they chose to get out and simply sit on cash. They tried to time the market, as opposed to trying to allocate properly around the three worlds of money.

Proper diversification can position clients to avoid a loss of more than an acceptable portion of their portfolios during a steep market decline. And, while diversification can't ensure a profit or that you won't lose money, it can help smooth out the volatility.

Another directive we try to convey, as best as we can, is to stay away from the political and stick with the actionable.

Again, that's hard. We estimate that 80 to 90 percent of the people who consult with us about retirement planning are extremely concerned with politics. They notice, as do we, that when uncertainty swirls in Washington, it can lead to volatility in the market. When tensions ease, the markets often stabilize.

Of course, there will always be disagreement among politicians regarding tax codes, government spending, interest rates, unemployment rates, and the housing market, to name a few economic issues with perpetually hot buttons.

Regardless, we never want to make any knee-jerk reactions based on politics. We attempt to stay on top of political maneuverings, especially since clients watch how it is interpreted on the cable news channel of their choice, but we tend to believe it's usually a numbers aspect that drives the market more than other factors.

We also stress that, rather than fret over market returns and let your nerves convince you to get out, only to see the market perform well for another two to three years, it's better to establish a "sweet spot" by incorporating the three worlds of money. Use allocations in the alternative and protections worlds to find the right percentage to leave in the market based on your risk tolerance.

If the market collapses, like it did in 2008 with a decrease of almost 34 percent in the Dow that year, you could stand to lose a much smaller percentage of your portfolio, depending on your risk tolerance and what was allocated in the three worlds.[27]

---

[27] Kimberly Amadeo. The Balance. Dec. 14, 2019. "Stock Market Crash of 2008." https://www.thebalance.com/stock-market-crash-of-2008-3305535

CHAPTER 8

Our Founding Principle: Control Volatility

"I don't enjoy any kind of danger or volatility. I don't have that kind of 'I love the bad guys' thing. No, no thank you."

–Tina Fey

Despite all the innovative schemes football coaches devise to execute their offense, the favorite play of all is the simplest. When the quarterback takes the snap and kneels, a team has its opponent beat and is running out the clock.

We want to build written retirement plans for clients to make them realize they are in a victory formation, and, like the aforementioned football teams, defense is perhaps the most important tactic we have at our disposal.

During the initial meeting we conduct as part of the Retirement Roadmap Review, we outline how our financial values trend conservative. We want you to be sure-footed with your savings and capable of making your money last through retirement. We'll learn about you, your goals and concerns, and analyze your portfolio and perform what an auto mechanic would term a "deep diagnostic" of risks, costs, and income.

In the second meeting, we'll continue on the theme of conserving what you've already built.

When you're in retirement and you're taking out money from your portfolio, protecting what you have and controlling the volatility is most important. Even if that means you must sacrifice higher returns on investments.

We cannot stress this point enough, which is why we incorporate one of the most important steps in the Retirement Roadmap Review into the end of our second meeting. That session is when we mutually commit to follow a prescribed plan based on findings from the Portfolio Review.

Let's share an example based on a completely fictional character, Suzanne. Let's say she's gone through our Discovery Meeting, so, like a first date, we've gotten to know the basics about each other: we know her high-level finance concerns, and we have told her (in a broad sense) how we like to approach plan building.

Our second appointment would start with us reviewing the Discovery Meeting and then proceeding into different assessments involving risk, costs, income, Social Security, and annuities. So, let's go through the process, using the hypothetical Suzanne and her assets as a model.

GOALS AND CONCERNS

1) Suzanne's retirement is imminent. She doesn't have plans to continue working, so we can assume the money she has—about $2 million—is all the money she *will* have.

2) Suzanne wants to grow and protect her assets using tax-efficient investment vehicles. She wants to use her portfolio to create an income stream that will allow her to live comfortably without the risk of outliving her money.

3) Suzanne is a moderate investor. Reasonable rate of return = 12 percent. Amount comfortable losing in the market = 20 percent. Riskalyze score (our risk-assessment software) = 32.

4) Suzanne would like to put into place a tangible retirement income plan and estate documents for her future.

CURRENT PORTFOLIO

INVESTMENT TYPE	AMOUNT	%
Market Investments	$1,866,055	94%
Alternative Investments	$0	0%
Protection Investments	$116,451	6%
TOTALS	$1,982,506	100%

RISK EXERCISE

Based on the information Suzanne provided in the Discovery Meeting, we have prepared a risk exercise detailing seven potential portfolios—something we do with most everyone who comes in for their second meeting with us. Each is designed to take on additional risk, with gains and losses based on volatility experienced in the market this century.

RISK EXERCISE

When presented with the bar graphs on this chart, most of our clients choose Portfolio B, C, or D, because they have already concluded they do not want to assume considerable risk in their retirement savings.

Let's say Suzanne was most enamored with Portfolio C, which is designed to help prevent a loss annually of any more than $163,557 in the worst of times but will probably not gain any more than $327,113 in the best of times, based on her total portfolio value of about $2 million (obviously these are estimates only and we can't make any guarantees about the maximum gains or losses in a portfolio when it's invested in the markets). Global's team specifically uses a software with an algorithm that estimates the portfolio has a 99 percent probability of falling within those boundaries. By percentage within this portfolio, it's estimated Suzanne neither stands to lose more than 8.25 percent in a given year nor gain more than 16.5 percent.

At the bottom of the exercise are different pie charts that correspond with the proposed portfolios. Suzanne's choice of Portfolio C would execute a split between the three worlds of money as follows: Market: 35 percent; Protection: 45 percent; Alternative: 20 percent.

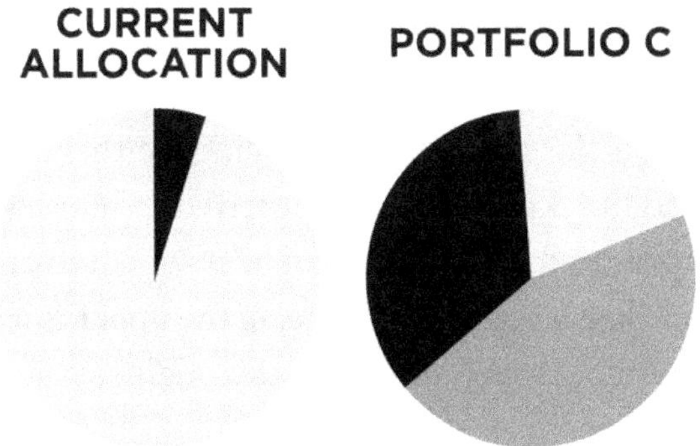

On the left is a pie chart that reflects our hypothetical Suzanne's current allocations, typical of many clients we bring on, which are mostly confined to the market and subject to enormous risk. On the right is the proposed "Portfolio C," which Suzanne has gravitated toward as being more in line with her speed of life.

STRESS TEST

What we often discover after showing prospective clients different portfolio examples, like we did during the risk exercise, is their tolerance for risk is actually less than they originally indicated.

We at Global Wealth Management use a computer simulation called "Riskalyze."

Remember, during the Discovery Meeting, Suzanne was willing to lose as much as 20 percent in the market. However, when asked to choose between the seven portfolio examples, let's say she chose Portfolio C, which attempts to limit loss to only 8.25 percent. This is something we see frequently with people we meet—they have a different idea of what they are comfortable with when we're talking about theoretical numbers, but putting it in terms of dollars and cents often yields a different reaction entirely.

The Riskalyze score represents risk on a scale from zero to one hundred. We like to think about it in terms of a speed limit—the faster you go, the more dangerous it gets. While most people shouldn't be too close to zero, not moving, neither should they be driving at the breakneck pace of nearly one hundred miles per hour. For Suzanne, it looks like she'd be most comfortable driving slightly faster than a residential zone, in the upper thirties. But her current portfolio is zooming on the highway in the sixties and seventies!

COST ANALYSIS

During this process, we discover both conventional fees and those hard-to-find fees.

We often find people aren't quite aware of what they are paying in fees for their portfolio and assets. Most people seem to be under the impression they pay just 1 or 2 percent, but we often find it may be double that once everyone from the advisor to the fund management company has taken their cut. Such discrepancies can result in higher costs that must be overcome in order to preserve retirement savings. No one wants excessive costs to potentially eat away at a portfolio.

Fees can be compared to an iceberg. Fees paid to an advisor are what you see on top of the water, since you can typically find these fees on your statement. What you don't see, which is part of the iceberg underneath the water, is the less visible fees inside mutual funds.

INCOME ANALYSIS

In this second meeting we show everyone their account aggregate snapshot. This shows Suzanne's portfolio asset's allocations, meaning how the money is divvied up into different products.

What we are most interested in talking about is what someone is earning in dividends and interest over the period of a year.

To put this into perspective, we equated the number to rental income. We say, "it's like you have a renter on everything in your portfolio (in Suzanne's case, we're talking about $2 million). The renter is paying you that percent (according to the account aggregate we mocked up for our hypothetical Suzanne, only $40,000 per year, or about 2 percent), which represents the income you earned as landlord. Now, let's consider how well everyone else on your block is doing. You're not going to like it if renters are paying those landlords more."

It would be possible for many people to improve on their earnings in a strong market. However, we cannot simply concentrate on good times, nor can we expect the market to soar steadily. We must also account for potential fluctuations and declines.

We want to get to where a person's yield, or "rental income" as we explained it, meets what they need to live off of every month, or at least close to it.

In the hypothetical case of Suzanne, she anticipates needing more than $40,000 a year from her 2 percent portfolio earnings. So, factoring in her Social Security checks and any optimization we could help her with there, she'll need closer to a 3 percent yield.

This is the point where we'd ask a real person, "Is that something you'd like us to help you fix?" Often their answer is a resounding "Yes!"

MONEY MAP

In this review, we'll show our Suzanne (we're starting to get attached to our hypothetical friend) a checklist of the issues we see with her current portfolio, as well as how we propose to address them.

For Suzanne, as with many of the real-life people we see in our office, the main problem is most of her assets are invested in the market.

When we looked at her risk analysis, it didn't tell us to drive like we're auditioning for NASCAR. We need allocations more representative of the three worlds of money: market, alternative, and protection.

Before we provide recommendations to Suzanne about the formal plan during her next visit (assuming she agrees to come on board as a client), we proceed with a mock exercise demonstrating the potential results due to the measures we will construct into a written retirement plan.

This is where the discussion truly gets to the heart of what we do as conservative financial retirement advisors.

PORTFOLIO EXERCISE

A further explanation regarding the perils of risk is appropriate at this juncture, complete with a definition of financial risk by the Financial Industry Regulatory Authority (FINRA):

All investments carry some degree of risk. Stocks, bonds, mutual funds, and exchange-traded funds can lose value, even all their value, if market conditions sour. Even conservative, insured investments, such as certificates of deposit (CDs) issued by a bank or credit union, come with inflation risk. They may not earn enough over time to keep pace with the ever-increasing cost of living.

Industry professionals often cite stock returns with a single number: the average. But, an average doesn't tell you about that factor we try to control for: volatility. We input the value of Suzanne's portfolio and show how it might have performed in the market based on fluctuations in the S&P 500 index. We put the numbers in with the beginning of the century (the year 2000) as the starting point and then show what a portfolio looks like, broken down into every succeeding year.

Stocks are particularly noteworthy for the level of risk they present. But, it's not just the stock market's movement that matters—it's often the market's movements in relation to your personal retirement timing. Most people have a good general understanding of the market's twists and turns, but the following exercise often surprises people when we illustrate the difference time and timing make.

If we input Suzanne's portfolio value as a beginning balance (in this case, we rounded to $1.8 million), we see that, had that amount been invested in 2000, she would have gained 6.43 percent over time. Obviously, Suzanne did not have that kind of money to invest that long ago, but just follow along for illustrative purposes. In this fictional example, Suzanne would have had to dismiss the down years (2000-02) that started this period. The same would have been true in 2008. But had she sat and done nothing, her $1.8 million would be worth $4,437,133 at the end of 2018, based on total earnings of 6.43 percent (for the sake of the illustration, we're not factoring in taxes or fees that may have resulted from these funds either way).

This illustration started out with those terrible years of the early aughts, so what if we reverse our illustration and the fictional Suzanne has all those bad years at the end instead? We invert the entire timetable, so the closing stretch now reflects the decline the market experienced from 2000-02. The end result? Precisely the same. In the case of Suzanne, her $1.8 million initial investment, left untouched, would have gained 6.43 percent and left her with $4.4 million. This is simply how the math works—forward or backward, so to speak. This is how averages perform.

However, once Suzanne begins taking income, it's a whole different story.

This comparative illustration sets up a key point we strive to make, which is: Everything changes when you begin withdrawing income from your portfolio.

We are ingrained to believe that strong returns are most critical when we are investing. And, that's true. But, when the situation changes for retirees, as they begin taking withdrawals from investments to provide them income, the most important factor we stress is controlling volatility.

To show this, we move on to our next set of examples, where we begin withdrawing income at a rate of $90,000 per year (5 percent of the initial $1.8 million outlay), an amount we chose to help with our imaginary illustration.

Suzanne

$1.8 million invested in S&P 500-like fund, December 1999 to December 2019, with $90,000 annual withdrawal

Year	Beginning Value	Annual Index Return	Account Value Change	Annual Withdrawal
2000	$1,800,000	-13.03%	-$234,540	$90,000
2001	$1,475,460	-23.34%	-$344,372	$90,000
2002	$1,041,088	26.36%	$274,431	$90,000
2003	$1,225,518	8.99%	$110,174	$90,000
2004	$1,245,692	2.97%	$36,997	$90,000
2005	$1,192,690	13.62%	$162,444	$90,000
2006	$1,265,134	3.53%	$44,659	$90,000
2007	$1,219,793	-38.49%	-$469,498	$90,000
2008	$660,295	23.48%	$155,037	$90,000
2009	$725,332	12.83%	$93,060	$90,000
2010	$728,392	0.00%	$0	$90,000
2011	$638,392	13.35%	$85,225	$90,000
2012	$633,617	29.59%	$187,487	$90,000
2013	$731,105	11.36%	$83,053	$90,000
2014	$724,158	-0.73%	-$5,286	$90,000
2015	$628,872	9.54%	$59,994	$90,000
2016	$598,866	19.44%	$116,420	$90,000
2017	$625,286	-6.25%	-$39,080	$90,000
2018	$496,205	6.59%	$32,700	$90,000
2019	$438,905	30.43%	$133,559	$90,000
2020	$482,464			

Suzanne			
$1.8 million invested in S&P 500-like fund, December 1999 to December 2019 return reversed, with $90,000 annual withdrawal			
Year	Beginning Value	Annual Index Return	Account Value Change	Annual Withdrawal
2019	$1,800,000	30.43%	$547,740	$90,000
2018	$2,257,740	6.59%	$148,785	$90,000
2017	$2,316,525	-6.25%	-$144,783	$90,000
2016	$2,081,742	19.44%	$404,691	$90,000
2015	$2,396,433	9.54%	$228,620	$90,000
2014	$2,535,053	-0.73%	-$18,506	$90,000
2013	$2,426,547	11.36%	$275,656	$90,000
2012	$2,612,202	29.59%	$772,951	$90,000
2011	$3,295,153	13.35%	$439,903	$90,000
2010	$3,645,056	0.00%	$0	$90,000
2009	$3,555,056	12.83%	$456,114	$90,000
2008	$3,921,170	23.48%	$920,691	$90,000
2007	$4,751,861	-38.49%	-$1,828,991	$90,000
2006	$2,832,869	3.53%	$100,000	$90,000
2005	$2,842,870	13.62%	$387,199	$90,000
2004	$3,140,069	2.97%	$93,260	$90,000
2003	$3,143,329	8.99%	$282,585	$90,000
2002	$3,335,914	26.36%	$879,347	$90,000
2001	$4,125,261	-23.34%	-$962,836	$90,000
2000	$3,072,425	-13.03%	-$400,337	$90,000
2020	$2,582,088			

Keep in mind, it isn't possible to invest in an index itself. Also, these figures don't reflect investment fees or taxes, which would reduce the values shown here.

Without making any changes and allowing the same withdrawals each year, beginning in 2000, the same startup figure of $1.8 million is reduced to under $500,000 by 2020. Almost all of Suzanne's retirement savings have disappeared under this scenario. She would not have even capitalized on the longest bull run in history, which included the highest close ever for the Dow Jones Industrial Average—26,828 on October 3, 2018.[28]

Conversely, if the script is flipped again, and the ups and downs of the S&P 500 index are reversed for that same period (2000-18), Suzanne would have gained money on her investment, and her total would have climbed to more than $2.5 million. In both cases, the average return was 6.43 percent just like in the previous set of examples.

By turning the market upside down to provide a make-believe example, results were not nearly as volatile for Suzanne. The steep decline that actually happened in 2008 is now reflected in our fictional 2010 (the tenth year of returns), and came after a ten-year period of steady growth. Even the three-year downturn experienced from 2000 to 2002 was not as destructive, though Suzanne's account still suffered considerable losses at the tail end of the "flipped script" example. At no point did the $90,000 withdrawal burn the principle. While it would not feel good to dip to $2.3 million in 2018 from $4.1 million in 2015, the losses still do not prompt outright lifestyle changes.

---

[28] Anne Sraders. TheStreet.com. December 17, 2018. "The Longest Bull Market: History and Facts in 2018." https://www.thestreet.com/investing/longest-bull-market-14804308

These examples help to define what is at the core of what Global Wealth Management believes in—implementing strategies to help manage volatility. However, we're incapable of simply turning the market upside down or sprinkling pixie dust on a portfolio to make it perform well.

The point here is having all of one's assets in the market subjects your income and the sustainability of your portfolio to the whims of market volatility. You better hope your first few years of income withdrawals happen when the market is flush with cash, or your later years could be quite diminished. This is why we recommend having a portfolio that protects a significant portion of your income in products with some kind of reliability.

We can't just concentrate on returns. We have to make controlling volatility our No. 1 objective.

****

Let's recall Portfolio C, the choice Suzanne made during the Risk Exercise phase of this second consultation between her and the team at Global Wealth Management.

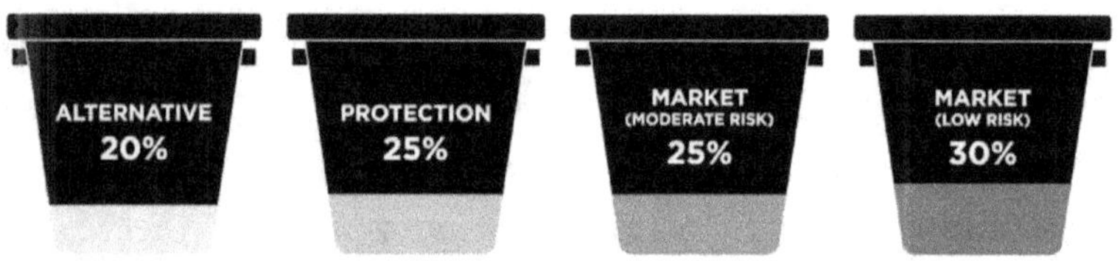

The illustration contains four asset classes to address the market, alternative, and protection components that best reflect ratios inherent to Portfolio C.

The first bucket represents a collection of alternative investments, which represents 20 percent of the portfolio.

Alternative investments, such as real estate investment trusts, are not immune to risk but also have no correlation to the market.

The second bucket (25 percent) contains a protection piece and acts similarly to the foundation of a home because the product is considered structurally sound. Here we may use annuities, certificates of deposit, or other investments guaranteed by governments, banks, insurance companies, etc.

The third bucket (25 percent) is market portfolios. They contain more risk.

The fourth bucket (30 percent) is an additional market portfolio, though it is considered a more moderate investment and not subject to as much market volatility.

The illustration still reflects the same $90,000 annual withdrawal for income and, in the end, after 2018, shows a balance of $2,382,166. In this example, Suzanne would actually have gained on her initial investment of $1.8 million. That's far better than being left with less than $500,000 and feeling forced to implement lifestyle changes.

At this point, with a real individual or couple, we'd begin discussing the particulars of becoming their formal advisor and preparing for the presentation of the full, written retirement plan in the third phase of the Retirement Roadmap Review.

CHAPTER 9

Maintaining Your Steady March: A Word on Annuities

"The pessimist complains about the wind; the optimist expects it to change; the realist adjusts the sails."

−William Arthur Ward

Annuities are not for everyone.

Now, with that stipulated, there has been tremendous demand within America's annuity base. About $240 billion—yes, billion, with a B—went into annuities in 2019. Of those, the sale of fixed annuities reached a record $139 billion.[29]

Our opinion on this development is two-fold.

First, more and more Americans are retiring. About 10,000 baby boomers are leaving the workforce each day, on average.[30] Many of them lost chunks of their life savings in 2001 to 2002,

---

[29] Jaqueline Sergeant. Financial Advisor. March 17, 2020. "2019 Annuity Sales Hit Highest Level Since '08." https://www.fa-mag.com/news/2019-annuity-sales-rose-to-highest-level-in-more-than-a-decade-54684.html

[30] Adam Bergman. Forbes. June 21, 2018. "Social Security Feels Pinch As Baby Boomers Clock Out For Good." https://www.forbes.com/sites/greatspeculations/2018/06/21/social-security-feels-pinch-as-baby-boomers-clock-out-for-good/

built their portfolios back up, and lost a portion again in 2008. Now, they're finally getting to retirement. They can't afford (nor do they want) that desperate feeling of watching their savings fragment again.

One of the most important considerations when choosing an annuity is the strength of the insurance company that stands behind the annuity. Contractual guarantees are only as sound as the insurance company selling the product. Rating agencies—A.M. Best, Moody's, and S&P—issue letter grades to the 2,000-plus insurance companies issuing annuities in the United States.

Some annuities tend to provide some upside, with little downside risk. Not a lot of products will do that. So, annuities have created something of a protection component.

Another reason we've seen a lot more demand in annuities is people are retiring more and more without the old corporate pension. A properly structured annuity with an income benefit will, whether you're eighty, ninety, or one hundred and ten years old, continue to pay you money. Many people are looking to create a guaranteed lifetime income they can count on.

So then, two reasons why people might consider an annuity:

- They desire a stabilization benefit they can't lose as part of their portfolio, but they want the potential for more growth than just leaving their money in bank accounts.
- They want to create, within a portion of their portfolio, a guaranteed income stream they can count on.

Now, if those two elements—stabilization and guaranteed income—aren't important, you probably don't want to own an annuity. But, if those elements are important to you, it may be worth investigating if this versatile product is a candidate for a portion of your portfolio.

GWM Primer on Four Basic Types of Annuities

Annuities were not created by Alfred Hitchcock. Nonetheless, these financial products are perhaps the most mysterious financial product we work with. Even clients who recognize the word "annuity" often do not have a strong understanding of the product.

So then, let's take a crack at unraveling a bit of the mystery.

What is an annuity, you ask? An annuity is basically an insurance product that pays out income. Here's how an annuity works: You make a premium payment or series of premium payments into the annuity, and it then makes payments to you at a future date or series of dates. The income you receive from an annuity can be distributed monthly, quarterly, annually, or even in a lump-sum payment. The size of your payments is determined by a variety of factors, including the length of your payment period. You can opt to receive payments for the rest of your life or for a set number of years.

Following are brief descriptions of the four basic types of annuities:

IMMEDIATE

Immediate annuities require a lump sum upfront and rely on annuitization to provide income immediately. Once income payments are received, access to the lump sum cannot be gained. Upon death, any remaining contract value is generally forfeited to the insurance company.

For this reason, they are often not as popular as other types of annuities. All other annuity contract types are "deferred," allowing you to fund your policy as a lump sum or over a period of years. You allow the policy the opportunity to grow over time, sometimes even years or decades.

One option with an immediate annuity is the use of a period-certain component. Such a stipulation allows for payments made over a specific amount of time, such as ten to twenty years, rather than providing income for the rest of one's life.

VARIABLE

Variable annuities are both an insurance product and an investment sold by insurance companies through someone who is registered to sell investments. The insurance company pools the premiums it receives and invests them in options called sub-accounts, which in turn invest in the market, where money is subject to losses because of market declines.

The money is not only subject to market volatility, but its value is also subject to additional investment fees, management fees, and capital gains taxes. When income is received, the amount will be locked in according to the value of the contract.

FIXED

Fixed annuities involve the purchase of a contract with a guaranteed interest rate. Regular income payments will begin, when you are ready, at the payout rate the contract guarantees. Payments will continue for the rest of the annuitant's life and, if stipulated, for the life of a spouse. Fixed annuities typically offer fairly conservative interest rates, but they can provide a financial safety net for someone who lives a long life. The value of a fixed annuity is simple to calculate because of its general steadiness.

A deferred annuity might be good for people in their mid-fifties or older who are looking at retiring soon. Payments from a deferred annuity can be delayed indefinitely. For annuities purchased with after-tax funds, the interest earned during that time is tax-deferred until you are ready to start taking withdrawals.

FIXED INDEX

A fixed index annuity often attempts to strike a balance between risk and reward, offering greater growth potential than traditional fixed annuities but less growth potential than variable annuities. Rather than growing at a set interest rate, a fixed index annuity has the potential to grow within a range, based on the performance of an external market index, such as the S&P 500. Each year on the annuity anniversary, the insurance company will calculate potential interest based on the chosen index, subject to limits such as a cap, spread, or participation rate. For example, if a cap is imposed at 5 percent, that percentage will represent the maximum interest for that year, in the event the S&P 500 gains more than 5 percent.

If the S&P value gained 2 percent, the annuity value would receive a 2 percent interest credit. However, if the S&P value shows a market loss, the contract value would not decline accordingly but instead level off at a 0 percent floor. Fixed index annuities will not plummet because of market volatility but can produce conservative growth that may offer the potential to help offset the effects of inflation.

A fixed index annuity with a 50 percent participation rate, on the other hand, would result in an interest credit of 7.5 percent if the stock index rose 15 percent. If the participation rate is 80 percent, the credited interest would be 12 percent, though an additional cap of, say, 7 percent, would further reduce the credited interest.

With all annuities, any interest earned can accumulate tax-deferred, and you'll be taxed when you make withdrawals. If you withdraw money before age fifty-nine-and-one-half, you'll be subject to an additional 10 percent federal penalty. Like all financial products, annuities involve fees and charges, including surrender penalties for withdrawals in the early years of the contract, so annuities work best when you don't need access to the money until retirement.

****

As we stressed in Chapter 10, our approach to retirement planning is defined by attempts to control volatility.

Diversification alone doesn't guarantee a profit or that you won't sustain any losses. If your portfolio is diverse, you can potentially keep volatility at bay and still preserve some upside potential. In retirement, our goal for clients is to make it so the lows aren't as low and the highs aren't as high, but the opportunity for growth still exists.

This can be achieved with a mix of assets, which include stocks, bonds, annuities, cash, and other alternatives. Together, the assets do not necessarily react to market conditions, trends, and swings in the same way.

Among many people we see, 2008 was a critical year. In a single day (September 29), the Dow Jones Industrial Average dropped 777.68 points, the largest point drop in history, until two dates in February 2018 closed worse.[31] While the total decline during that market drop was not the worst nosedive in history by percentage, it was a trend that rocked many of the retirees we have advised in the years since.

---

[31] Kimberly Amadeo. The Balance. Nov. 6, 2018. "Stock Market Crash of 2008, Follow the Timeline to Understand Why It Crashed." https://www.thebalance.com/stock-market-crash-of-2008-3305535

That unfortunate downturn in 2008 emphasizes the need for them to incorporate safety provisions into a sound retirement plan. They lived it. Most lost money during that period. Some lost considerable amounts.

We see the effects elsewhere, too. Following that 2008 market collapse, interest rates on home loans dropped to advantageous levels for consumers. Many refinanced their homes at the lower rates. For many of those who did so, one tradeoff was to catch up on retirement savings lost by devoting more money into the 401(k) plan or IRA after taking out a new mortgage with a lower payment. Some, however, now find themselves carrying a mortgage into retirement.

This was the case for Ed and Mary. The two booked an appointment after attending one of our dinner seminars.

Ed was a marine biologist, and Mary was a hospital dietician. Both had a decent knowledge of financial instruments but not a complete understanding. They knew of the market fallout in 2008 and how it negatively impacted their retirement savings. They also were not big fans of annuities, based on sentiments expressed by friends and family members they had leaned on previously for occasional financial pointers.

The couple had rebounded nicely from the 2008 collapse. Ten years later, they wanted to at least begin planning for retirement while considering options for how soon to leave the workforce, depending on different financial factors. Yet, they were not in a position where they wanted to pay off their low-interest mortgage.

Although Ed and Mary expressed reservations regarding annuities, we told them, for retirees who need a constant stream of dependable income, deferred income annuities may be a good option. For a lump-sum payment, some provide guaranteed monthly payments starting immediately. Others allow you to turn on the income stream at a predetermined date. They aren't something to allocate your entire nest egg to, but, for a portion of it, the protection provided by a guaranteed source of annuity income can be worthwhile.

You would not invest all of your portfolio into an annuity. But, for the right portion of your assets, properly constructed annuities can provide you a steady source of income for the rest of your life—one you literally cannot outlive.

CHAPTER 10

Post-Retirement: Lurking Presence of the RMD

"The question isn't at what age I want to retire, it's at what income."

–George Foreman

If reviewed as a purchase, retirement could well be the most expensive item you acquire in your life.

The savings you build through retirement plans could, and should, exceed other major purchases, such as vehicles, a college education, or even a house.

Even your Social Security benefits are only based on taxes you paid into that program. A pension is different, though few Americans in the private sector rely exclusively on such retirement income.

In 2018, just 4 percent of private sector workers counted on a defined-benefit pension plan as their only retirement account. In the early 1960s, 60 percent of private sector workers counted on pensions as their income source in retirement. Industries with a strong union presence are most likely the only ones who still have employers that offer traditional pensions. Most often, deals have been negotiated by those employers to reduce or eliminate (pension) plans.[32]

We want to remind you again: Your diligence toward saving for retirement through a 401(k) plan is to be commended and recommended—particularly since almost one in five future retirees in America feel as if they will never be ready to retire, according to a 2018 survey Harris Poll compiled for Nationwide Retirement Institute.[33]

Dollar-Cost Averaging

One characteristic you learn when investing for the long term is dollar-cost averaging. You consistently place money into your 401(k), so, when the market trends upward, your investments can increase and your assets build. Yet, even when the market declines, those dollars you allocate in your company plan enable you to buy more shares at a lower price. At some point, the market will likely recover, and the value of your shares will expand and possibly be more valuable than before. It's not guaranteed to ensure a profit or prevent you from losing money, but the concept of dollar-cost averaging is a time-tested strategy to help smooth out volatility in a portfolio.

Exercise caution, however, with the concept of dollar-cost averaging in retirement. While earning money during your work career, you could shop for "bargains" when the market lagged. During such times, the dollars you contributed to your 401(k) bought more assets at a reduced price. In retirement, you are

---

[32] CNN Money. 2018. "Ultimate guide to retirement: Just how common are defined benefit plans?"
https://money.cnn.com/retirement/guide/pensions_basics.moneymag/index7.htm
[33] Harris Poll. Nationwide Mutual Insurance Company. November 2019. "Nationwide Retirement Institute Tax Efficient."
Retirement Income https://nationwidefinancial.com/media/pdf/NFM-18922AO.pdf

selling assets to create income needed in retirement. More assets must be sold in a down market to make the same amount of money you made in a market that trended upward.

The Tax Crunch

While you accumulate wealth, the primary message for those participating in 401(k) plans is to save as much as possible and at least attempt to allocate the percentage of salary needed to attain the full match offered by an employer.

However, you need to be aware that any pre-tax contribution you make into your 401(k) or IRA is not tax-free. It is tax-deferred. Big difference.

Unfortunately, a 2018 survey Harris Poll conducted for Nationwide Retirement Institute revealed nearly half (47 percent) of recent retirees wished they better understood how their income in retirement is taxed.[34]

Very rarely is anything free of taxation. Using 401(k)s and IRAs in retirement is no different. The taxes the government deferred when you were in your working years are now coming due, and you will pay taxes on that income at whatever your current tax rate is.

Although the rate of return was never guaranteed from your 401(k) or IRA, Uncle Sam makes sure to impose his own guarantee—to collect taxes.

The government has a required minimum distribution, or RMD, rule. Beginning at age seventy-two, you are required to withdraw a certain minimum amount every year from your 401(k) or IRA, or you will face a 50 percent tax penalty on any RMD monies you should have withdrawn but didn't, and that's on top of income tax. One potential concession is you will hopefully be

---

[34] Ibid.

in a lower tax bracket in your retirement years than the bracket you were in while working and earning paychecks.

Appraising the Required Minimum Distribution

Two sets of retirees essentially emerge when required minimum distributions must be taken.

The first set is composed of people who need their RMDs to live, whether the income is used to take a fun trip or used for day-to-day expenses.

The second set is composed of people who do not need their RMDs to facilitate their lifestyle.

Let's envision someone who would belong to that second category, who receives both a pension distribution and Social Security in retirement to augment a handsome portfolio. This retiree, whom we will call Don, has no debt.

Once clients turn seventy-two, reinvesting RMDs into tax beneficial retirement accounts is not allowed by the IRS, unless you are still working. Investment options that are often less volatile, such as bonds, money market accounts, and mutual funds, are possibilities for the money withdrawn to meet RMD requirements. However, gains made from these investments can result in taxable consequences.

Let's say our fictional character, Don, was interested in leaving a legacy to his loved ones. He thought to himself, "Why not use the money I withdraw for RMDs to fund a life insurance policy?"

Well, a policy in his name would be considered part of his estate. This would mean, when Don passed, his beneficiaries could be stuck paying additional estate taxes.

Don could transfer ownership of the life insurance policy to someone else. But, by doing so, he would no longer have control of beneficiaries and could no longer access money in the policy, functions referred to as "incidents of ownership." The IRS requires a policy must be transferred three years prior to Don's death for heirs to avoid estate taxes. Finally, Don could not name his wife as beneficiary to avoid estate taxes because proceeds she receives from the policy upon Don's death are considered part of the estate.

Concerns posed by the transfer rules prompted Don to consider an irrevocable life insurance trust (ILIT), which would serve as the owner of the life insurance policy.

Assets of an ILIT are no longer in the owner's name (in this case, Don) but instead become assets of the trust, which is named for an entity. The trust then becomes the beneficiary. Responsibility for managing funds, purchasing and holding policies, filing death claims, and making payments to surviving heirs becomes the responsibility of the trust's entity. It is managed by a trustee.

The policy's purchase would be attained by using Don's RMD allocations each year. Again, incidents of ownership apply. Changes allowing life insurance policies to be placed into an ILIT must be done irrevocably. This strategy works best if Don is healthy enough to qualify for life insurance and the premiums are affordable. If the RMD won't pay the full premium due, Don needs to determine if he's willing and able to use outside funds to help fund the policy. So, make sure to discuss this concept with a qualified advisor if it's something you're considering.

****

Now, let's address the other set of people we mentioned, those who need RMDs to meet monthly expenses . . .

It is wise to manage your cash flow and have money taken as RMDs deposited directly into a bank account.

This approach ensures you can take out the proper amount to fulfill the government rate for RMDs, so you can avoid a steep tax penalty (50 percent of the amount not taken on time) if you withdraw less money than Uncle Sam stipulates. If withdrawals are taken in an annual lump sum amount, it is important to remember the deadline is December 31.

The IRS has established divisors based on your age to use each year when determining your RMD. These are listed in the IRS Uniform Lifetime Table listed below. For example, if you are seventy-five and the balance of your IRA on December 31 of the previous year was $100,000, then you must withdraw at least 4,367 the following year ($100,000 divided by 22.9).

If you examine the following table, you'll notice the percentages the IRS applies to your IRA balance escalate each year once you begin having to withdraw money for RMDs.

For those who need RMDs to meet expenses in retirement, it is worthwhile to remember the perils of reverse dollar-cost averaging. If the market dips and you must take out RMDs, the sale of investments in a down market is something retirees often cannot recover from, since they are retired and no longer earning a paycheck.

This is an example of why it is critical in retirement to control volatility. We have seen clients who come to us in their early seventies who have already begun to take RMDs but are still depending on growth in their accounts to cover the withdrawals.

Others have come to us with money in CDs earning a small percentage while their RMDs require they take 4 or 5 percent of their savings. Unfortunately, it becomes altogether too clear they're just draining their accounts.

IRS Uniform Lifetime Table (for calculating RMDs)

Age	Distribution period	% of balance
70	27.4	3.65
71	26.5	3.77
72	25.6	3.91
73	24.7	4.05
74	23.8	4.20
75	22.9	4.37
76	22.0	4.55
77	21.2	4.72
78	20.3	4.93
79	19.5	5.13
80	18.7	5.35
81	17.9	5.59
82	17.1	5.85
83	16.3	6.13
84	15.5	6.45
85	14.8	6.76
86	14.1	7.09
87	13.4	7.46
88	12.7	7.87
89	12.0	8.33
90	11.4	8.77

CHAPTER 11

Get Smart: Attempt to Combat Taxes in Retirement

"A cloudy day at the beach is still a day at the beach."

–Anonymous

Caricatures drawn to depict Uncle Sam often reflect a bearded fellow waving an American flag—a symbolic tribute to patriotism.

Now, you may not relate taxes to patriotism. Taxes, however, attempt to cover the goods and services appropriated by federal, state, county, and municipal governments.

The payment of federal taxes is akin to Uncle Sam putting his flag down and extending an outstretched palm to taxpayers. Think of the iconic poster in which Uncle Sam points his finger with the statement, "I Want You." The message, originally intended for military recruitment, can also apply to taxes.

In retirement, that mission to collect a share of your savings is quite pronounced. No one, however, would consider you to be more patriotic if your tax payments exceeded your tax obligations.

One condition of the traditional 401(k) or IRA is the government requires you to withdraw a portion of your account beginning when you turn seventy-two.

Calculations based on the size of your account and your estimated lifespan then determine the extent of required minimum distributions (RMDs) you will pay for the rest of your life. This guarantees the government will receive taxes on the retirement accounts you built without paying taxes on the front end.

Goody, goody . . . right?

Such is life in America.

Beat Uncle Sam to the Punch: Convert to Roth

One potentially advantageous strategy is to run fast and avoid the tax hammer Uncle Sam starts swinging when you turn age seventy-two.

This can be achieved through conversions into a Roth IRA. With a Roth, taxes are paid on the front end. Thus, once your post-tax money is in the Roth account, and the rules and limitations of the account are followed (withdrawals are taken after age fifty-nine-and-one-half and the account is at least five years old), your distributions will no longer be taxed. No income tax is collected and required minimum distributions are not in effect.

Converting money saved in traditional IRAs to a Roth IRA is not a strategy we endorse for all our clients. In cases where a suitable retirement must be funded with money saved in traditional IRAs, it can be wise to keep those funds in those accounts. The money paid up front on the conversion requires time to marinate before any tax savings can be realized.

However, there are certain criteria that merit recommendation for a Roth conversion:

- If you don't expect to draw income from your IRA during your lifetime and you are in your early to mid-sixties, a conversion can enable you to avoid RMDs. Your savings can then be preserved for your beneficiaries. Taxes were paid up front, so heirs do not have to pay them later, making the conversion a solid legacy strategy.

If you are younger than fifty-nine-and-one-half, you can still make conversions into a Roth IRA without incurring the 10 percent early withdrawal penalty. That allows considerable time to make conversions before retirement, as long as you can allocate funds from outside of your retirement account to pay for the tax bite incurred with the conversion.

■ If you are in your seventies and already taking RMDs, it is still wise to consider a Roth conversion since your RMDs increase every year and you could live another twenty to thirty years based on increasing lifespans. An analysis can be conducted to properly evaluate the prospect of a conversion, something we do for clients as early as the initial Retirement Roadmap Review meeting.

Conversion calculators for Roth IRAs provide solid insight into whether a conversion is right for a particular client. The 2017 Tax Cuts and Jobs Act included reforms that incorporated lower individual tax rates. A stipulation in that legislation, however, dictates the rates expire in 2026, giving taxpayers a limited timeframe in which the conversion of funds contain a smaller tax penalty. This makes it paramount for anyone who is interested in being forward-thinking about their tax bill on a 401(k) or IRA to really consider a Roth conversion strategy so they can take full advantage of the federal tax rates before 2026.

While conversions may prove to be the right move for the future, the execution can be rough for those already on relatively tight budgets. Even if spread out over time, the money devoted to taxes can create shortfalls if people are not careful. The money used to cover those taxes should not be withdrawn from a retirement account. If those funds are in your traditional IRA, it is best to leave things alone.

Tax brackets can be difficult to predict, particularly twenty to thirty years out. However, if you sense you will be in a lower tax bracket in retirement, a conversion might not be a good option. Taxes would then be higher on the conversion than they will be when withdrawing from a traditional IRA in retirement.

For high earners who are not allowed to make direct contributions into a Roth, it could still be advantageous to convert money from a traditional IRA into a Roth. No income limits are stipulated for such conversions, and they can be processed at any age. The conversions can also be made over time to lessen the tax burden incurred with the conversion.

In 2020, the contribution limit into a Roth IRA was $6,000 for those under fifty and $7,000 for those over fifty. Single filers must have a modified adjusted gross income of less than $137,000 to make contributions, with contributions reduced beginning at $122,000. For those married filing jointly, a modified adjusted gross income must be less than $203,000, with contributions reduced beginning at $193,000.

Never forget, Uncle Sam's hand is always extended when it comes to taxes. Political maneuverings provide no assurances of what could happen in the future, though one landmark, the National Debt Clock near Times Square in New York, provides an ominous indicator.

The gross national debt, in mid-2020, tallied more than $26 trillion.[35] Calculatorsite.com reported a stack of $100 bills would stretch 11,995 miles in order to equal $20 trillion. A trillion, by the

---

[35] US Debt Clock. July 9, 2020. https://www.usdebtclock.org/

way, contains twelve zeroes and is equal to one million dollars multiplied by one million.[36]

FIUL Strategies Can Help with Taxes

If designed properly, a fixed indexed universal life insurance policy potentially offers a favorable tax advantage in addition to the traditional death benefit it provides.

The ability to potentially withdraw the cash value of your policy without paying income taxes, even on the accumulation, can be an advantageous method to avoid the kind of tax issues that particularly strike a large IRA.

Like any permanent insurance, an FIUL policy will remain in force as long as you continue to pay premiums. If your cash value is sufficient, you can borrow against your policy's cash value, income tax-free.[37] Obviously, when some clients hear it's insurance, they balk at the idea. Often, they recall a point in their lives when they dealt with a pushy agent, and they aren't interested in reliving the experience.

We stress that an FIUL is an insurance product, so health factors will be assessed to determine qualifications for those who apply for such policies.

---

[36] Becky Kleanthous. thecalculatorsite.com. Aug. 3, 2018. "How Much is a TRILLION?" https://www.thecalculatorsite.com/articles/finance/how-much-is-a-trillion.php

[37] Policy loans will reduce available cash values and death benefits and may cause the policy to lapse or may affect any guarantees against lapse. Additional premium payments may be required to keep the policy in force. In the event of a lapse, outstanding policy loans in excess of unrecovered cost basis will be subject ordinary income tax. Policy loans are not usually subject to income tax unless the policy is classified as a modified endowment contract (MEC) under IRC Section 7702A. However, withdrawals or partial surrenders from a non-MEC policy are subject to income tax to the extent that the amount distributed exceeds the owner's cost basis in the policy. Loans, withdrawals, or partial surrenders from an MEC policy are subject to income tax to the extent of any gains in the policy, and, if the payment occurs prior to age fifty-nine-and-one-half, a 10 percent federal additional tax may apply.

In the case of life insurance, a section in the U.S. tax code (7702) stipulates it is permissible for funds inside a life insurance policy to accumulate tax-free and later provide a death benefit to benefactors, also tax-free.

So then, what makes the FIUL particularly attractive for some? The index component. The potential to accumulate cash value through interest credits based on the performance of an external index, without ever being invested in the market itself, makes it more appealing. An index is a tool used to measure the stock market, like the S&P 500 or Dow Jones Industrial.

You can't invest directly into an index. Rather, it's sort of a ruler. With an FIUL policy, your potential cash accumulation interest credits are based on an index, with what is called a "floor" and a "cap." That means, if the chosen market index does well, your contract will be credited interest on the cash accumulation based on whatever your policy's index is, up to the policy's cap. This calculation is done once each year, on your policy anniversary. If the market has a bad year and the index shows negative gains, your account still gets credited whatever is your contract floor, which is typically around 0 to 2 percent depending on the policy you select.

This feature removes much of the volatility that makes the market an unstable mechanism that truly stings whenever it goes bust. The policy's guarantees protect your money during market declines. Best yet, it is relatively easy to understand.

It might still be a little confusing, so here's an example. Let's say your contract cap is 12.5 percent and the floor is 0 percent. If the market returns 20 percent, your contract value gets a 12.5 percent interest credit. The next year, the S&P 500 returns a negative 26 percent. The insurance company won't credit your policy anything, but you also won't see your policy value slip because of that negative performance (although policy charges and expenses will still be deducted from your policy).

So, your policy won't lose value because of poor market conditions, but you can still stand to realize higher interest credits due to market gains. The following chart illustrates a hypothetical FIUL policy using the S&P 500. As you can see, because of the cap, the FIUL doesn't have the sharp upticks of the index, but it also never goes down due to market losses.

An FIUL has the potential to balance both protection and growth. Also, the potential cash accumulation is a real draw here for people who want protection from market losses, potential growth, and a death benefit for their beneficiaries.

Some people choose to overfund their policies and borrow against their cash values to help provide supplemental retirement income. This might be a good move for you, but, keep in mind, policy loans will reduce available cash values and death benefits and may cause the policy to lapse. Additional premium payments may be required to keep the policy in force.

It is possible to overfund the policy cash value in the first five or ten years and then potentially not have to pay any more money into the policy, letting the cash accumulation self-fund the policy. However, when overfunding an FIUL policy, it is important to understand the policy may become a modified endowment contract, or MEC, if premium payments exceed certain amounts specified under the Internal Revenue Code.

This can happen if a policy has been funded too quickly in its early years. For policies determined to be MECs, distributions during the life of the insured, including loans, are fully taxable as income to the extent there is a gain in the policy over the amount of net premiums paid. An additional 10 percent federal income tax may apply for withdrawals made prior to age fifty-nine-and-one-half. In addition, FIUL involves surrender penalties for withdrawals in the early years of the policy.

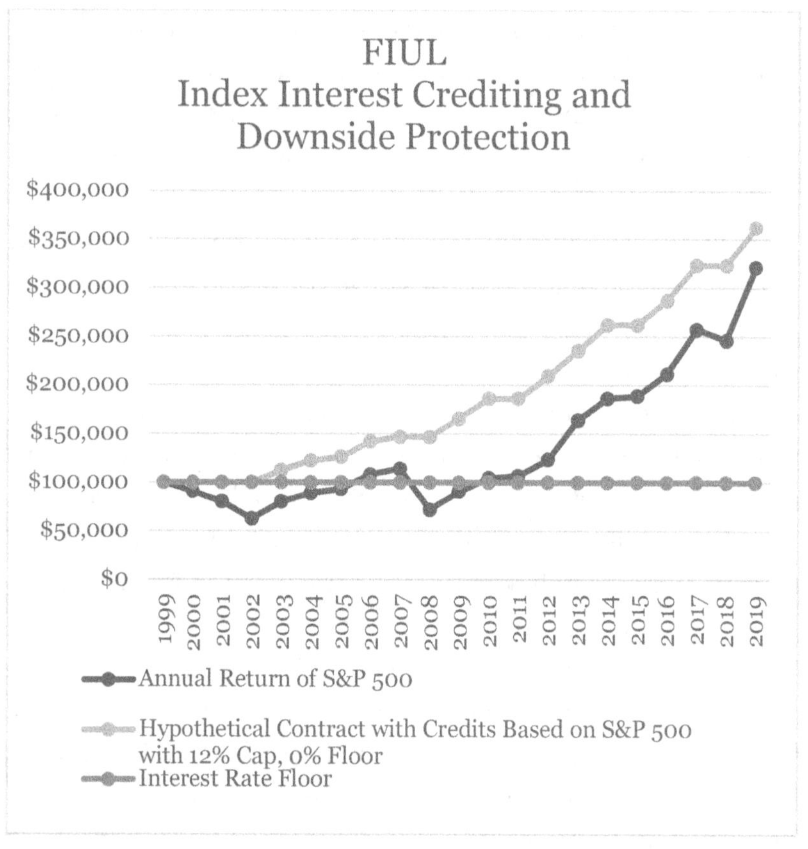

Preceding is a hypothetical illustration of the following:[38]

1. The top line, lightest in color, represents FIUL policy with an index interest crediting method tied to the performance of the S&P 500 index. It assumes a hypothetical cap rate of 12.5 percent and an interest rate floor of 0 percent.

---

[38] Standard & Poor's®, S&P® and S&P 500® are registered trademarks of Standard & Poor's Financial Services LLC. S&P 500® returns are based on information obtained from Yahoo Finance GSPC Historical Prices and StandardandPoors.com

2. The second, darkest line represents the S&P 500 index, including dividends.
3. The straight line represents the guaranteed interest rate floor.

There's a lot going on with these policies. If you don't take the time to understand the basics of how they work, it's entirely possible to fall behind on premium payments and end up with a policy that lapses. Yet, if you understand the terms of your contract and are working with purpose, an FIUL could be a powerful cog in the greater mechanics of your overall retirement strategy.

Municipal Bonds Provide Another Tax Strategy

Another investment vehicle that can provide a tax advantage is municipal bonds. States, cities, or counties issue municipal bonds to fund public projects. The interest is tax-free at the federal level. If the bonds were issued in the state you call home, taxes also are not levied locally or at the state level.

So, how much savings can a municipal bond provide? Well, when compared to a corporate bond, the savings can be significant. If you are taxed at a 25 percent rate on your federal return, $100 in interest on a corporate bond would be subject to a 25 percent tax that allows you to retain $75. A $100 interest return on a municipal bond can be pocketed entirely.

Keep in mind, however, corporate bonds often offer interest rates more favorable than comparably rated municipal bonds. In some instances, the tax crunch levied on the corporate bonds may not completely negate the returns, resulting in a higher yield (even after the tax deduction) than the tax-free municipal bond.

Gains on the sale of municipal bonds are subject to capital gains taxes if sold at a price higher than the purchase price. By holding the bond for more than a year, the tax imposed will be the more favorable long-term capital gains rate.

Typically, clients with a higher net worth can find more value using a tax-free strategy involving municipal bonds. Often, such clients have other investments generating dividends and interest, so, for a portion of their portfolios, it is good to incorporate the tax-free nature municipal bonds provide. Usually the clients we see who benefit from that component have a couple million dollars or more of investible assets.

One of the strategies popular with bonds is using "ladders," where each bond or bond fund is purchased for a period of time, allowing you to have "rungs" of income provided by strategic bond sales at different points in time, perhaps at intervals of five, ten, or fifteen years. If you can afford to have your money tied up in these investments over long periods of time (such as that), using the "rungs" of the bond ladder over time can provide somewhat of a hedge against the fluctuations of interest rates that often destabilize shorter term bonds or bond funds. As bonds are also generally more stable than stocks, this strategy can also provide a more regular alternative within a broader portfolio.

For some terminology within the bond world, here are some definitions to increase your understanding of them. The rate of interest a bond pays annually is the coupon rate. The rate of return it generates is its yield. The face value of the bond is its par value. A premium means purchasing a bond for more than its par value. A discount means purchasing a bond for less than its par value.

Something to note about municipal bonds is they can be misleading. People get hooked into coupon rates. They notice a bond has a 5 percent coupon rate and think they're going to get a 5 percent return on their money. That's not true. Bonds are traded on a premium, so their real return can be only 2 or 3 percent, because typically they have to pay a premium for the bond.

Anyone considering the purchase of a bond should become educated on how bonds work. Depending on economic factors, you might not be getting the return you think you are, but sometimes bond brokers, in order to make a living, are not going to tell you that.

CHAPTER 12

The State of Your Health

"Never give up, for that is just the place and time that the tide will turn."

–Harriet Beecher Stowe

Chances are pretty good you have grown fatigued over the raging debate over health care that often dominates Washington politics. Issues that consistently arise on the state and municipal levels can grow tedious, too.

At this point a simple reference to something as contentious as "Obamacare," "repeal and replace," or something as specific as pre-existing conditions or network providers can make your eyes roll to some extent, especially when subjected to political spin.

In the end, however, the question over who is going to pay for health care is the one in which the consumer is most interested. Certainly, cost factors related to health care are a huge concern for those in retirement or approaching retirement, just like they are for virtually any adult in our society.

The most recent study conducted by Centers for Medicare and Medicaid Services revealed health care spending in the United States grew 4.6 percent in 2018, to $3.6 trillion or $11,172 per person, and accounted for 17.7 percent of the Gross Domestic

Product.[39] The staggering cost of health care, or its unavailability, contributed to 8.5 percent of Americans (27.5 million) not having health insurance at any point in 2018.[40]

One of our responsibilities at Global Wealth Management is to keep apprised of various health issues and help clients fund a sensible approach to securing health care in retirement. Some general considerations are in order regarding what you could face when calculating health care costs.

One sobering point: Fidelity Investments estimated, in 2018, $280,000 in after-tax savings will be needed for the average couple to meet medical expenses in retirement. That estimate does not account for inflation and excludes long-term care.[41]

MEDICARE

Once you turn sixty-five, Medicare is considered your primary source of health insurance, regardless of whether you have applied. Also, understand that you should apply once the initial enrollment period begins, three months before you turn sixty-five. The period ends three months after the month you turn sixty-five. Failure to act during this period could result in a penalty.

---

[39] CMS.gov. Centers for Medicare and Medicaid Services. Dec. 17, 2019. https://www.cms.gov/Research-Statistics-Data-and-Systems/Statistics-Trends-and-Reports/NationalHealthExpendData/NationalHealthAccountsHistoricalhttps://www.cms.gov/research-statistics-data-and-systems/statistics-trends-and-reports/nationalhealthexpenddata/nationalhealthaccountshistorical.html

[40] Associated Press. Sept. 10, 2019. "Number of Americans without health insurances rises for 1st time in a decade." nbcnews.com. https://www.nbcnews.com/politics/politics-news/number-americans-without-health-insurance-rises-1st-time-decade-n1052016l

[41] Fidelity Investments. April 18, 2018. "Tab for your health care post-age 65? Try $280,000 for the average couple." https://www.fidelity.com/viewpoints/personal-finance/plan-for-rising-health-care-costs

Something to be aware of if you retire before turning sixty-five is the coverage gap in health insurance you will face. Health care is an expense that sometimes deters those who want to retire early. Often, they decide the coverage they receive through their employer is just too good to give up.

We can review the prospect of any gap in health insurance coverage and explore possibilities to determine recommended amounts to set aside for future health care. Also, it is appropriate to assess any medical needs that may require coverage in addition to Medicare once you qualify at age sixty-five for that program.

Following are the different "parts" of Medicare and what they do.

PART A

Labeled in general as the hospital insurance component of Medicare, Part A covers:

- Inpatient care in a hospital
- Skilled nursing facility care
- Inpatient care in a skilled nursing facility (not custodial or long-term care)
- Hospice care
- Home health care

Medicare.gov recommends most people enroll in Part A when they turn sixty-five, even if they have health insurance from an employer. Most people don't pay a monthly premium for Part A since they were charged Medicare taxes during their work careers.

PART B

Labeled in general as the medical insurance component of Medicare, Part B covers:

- Clinical research
- Ambulance services
- Durable medical equipment
- Mental health: inpatient, outpatient, partial hospitalization
- Second opinion regarding surgery
- Limited outpatient prescription drugs

A monthly premium is charged for Part B. In 2019, the standard premium was $135.50, but the premium varies depending on your income and when you enroll in Part B.

Retirement Sure Seems to Suit You . . . But What if You Need Long-Term Care?

The cost of long-term care is significant. Attempting to cover such costs within a financial retirement plan that also accounts for requisite income sometimes requires a substantial outlay of capital some feel is best left for the cost of living rather than the cost of dying.

The feeling is understandable. Retirees want to focus on what they can do and what they can get out of their remaining years. It's important for you to attempt to realize those ambitions, and, again, it is why we go to great lengths to listen to your vision for retirement.

It is disturbing, however, that six out of ten Americans refuse to accept they will ever require long-term care. Also, two-thirds of respondents in a 2017 Cost of Care Study conducted by Genworth Financial expected long-term care costs to be covered either in part, or completely, by government programs.[42]

---

[42] Genworth Financial. Sept. 26, 2017. "Genworth 2017 Annual Cost of Care Survey: Costs Continue to Rise Across All Care Settings."
http://newsroom.genworth.com/2017-09-26-Genworth-2017-Annual-Cost-of-Care-Survey-Costs-Continue-to-Rise-Across-All-Care-Settings

Provisions differ among long-term care insurance policies, but a diagnosis of some type of dementia can often trigger the payment of benefits.

Another qualification is the inability to perform two of six activities of daily living (ADLs)—eating, bathing, dressing, toileting, maintaining continence, and transferring (getting in and out of bed) without assistance. These are considered markers of our own independence and the ability to take care of ourselves.

Other functions, such as managing medications, doing laundry, and shopping are also considered skills needed to live independently. In-home assistance is often the first step taken to help someone who cannot perform all activities or skills based on a functional assessment.

Again, we understand reservations clients have in devoting a considerable amount of hard-earned savings toward long-term needs they may never encounter. We understand how people are sometimes inclined to roll the dice and convince themselves they have already led a long, healthy life—why believe that may change?

Note, however, recipients of long-term care are getting younger. In 2010, respondents in the Genworth survey indicated 81 percent of care recipients were sixty-five or older. In the 2018 survey, care recipients dropped to 57 percent who were sixty-five or older.[43]

Obviously, aging can have a dramatic effect—not only on a person who is, say, afflicted with the loss of memory and cognitive functions, but also on the person, usually a loved one, who is left to be a caregiver in such situations.

---

[43] Genworth Financial. "Cost of Care Survey: How caregiving impacts families, communities and society, Beyond Dollars 2018."
https://mma.prnewswire.com/media/784202/Genworth_Beyond_Dollars_Study_201 8_Executive_Summary.pdf?p=pdf

Imagine if the caregiver is subjected to a lengthy period in which his or her life is devoted primarily to, say, a spouse afflicted with Alzheimer's disease.

The toll is immeasurable. The loved one you vowed to hold until death-do-you-part could become a shell of their former self. Riddled by a debilitating and indiscriminate disease, that person no longer shows an ability to even recognize you.

A child who is obligated to care for a parent can also struggle with the emotional toll. In addition, the child's livelihood can be adversely impacted if time is missed at work. Income and work performance can be affected and financial health lowered, especially if savings are depleted. Depression can also hinder the caregiver's personal health.

Heartbreaking . . . and yet we have seen these scenarios play out many times. Agony and pain can be almost unbearable when caring for a loved one who no longer recognizes you and can no longer communicate with you. Caregivers desperately need breaks just to get out, be active, interact with others, and gain some relief from work. Yet, if the funding does not exist for a modest level of home health care, even a brief respite could be impossible.

Therefore, it is important to stress this: Long-term care planning is not just about the person covered in a policy. The hardship placed on loved ones—a spouse, a child, even a friend—can be significant without the resources necessary to provide capable outside assistance. The role of caregiving, quite frankly, is a commitment few people are adequately prepared to perform.

Of respondents who participated in the 2018 Cost of Care Survey conducted by Genworth, 82 percent conveyed positive feelings from providing care, but 52 percent conceded they did not feel qualified to provide physical care. Respondents also acknowledged high levels of stress (53 percent) and feelings of depression (41 percent).[44]

****

The prospect of an insurer attempting to sell someone long-term care insurance (LTCI) has dwindled in recent years because many insurers have stopped offering the product. Expenses incurred by insurers caused some to back out of the LTCI business. Carriers who stopped selling policies were, in all likelihood, offering policies that were underperforming and were not realistically priced.

One of our financial retirement advisors at Global Wealth Management noticed the effect of escalating costs firsthand. A close relative purchased an LTCI policy when she was in her early fifties. When that person turned seventy, a notice was received stipulating the premium was being doubled to $10,000 per year, after paying $5,000 previously.

At that point, a difficult decision unfolds. The insured is tempted, of course, to say, "forget it," and cancel the policy. Yet, after paying a considerable amount on the policy for so many years and knowing the need for long-term care will become more probable because of aging, the insured may absorb the price hike and "keep paying for this thing because I've paid so much into it already."

Based on such situations, we advise clients with LTCI policies to understand their contract and ascertain if premiums can be raised. Realize, too, many traditional LTCI policies may pay benefits only if care is needed.

---

[44] Ibid.

An attractive alternative for many is an annuity with a long-term care rider. Such riders can prove advantageous compared to a sudden rise in premiums in traditional LTCI policies.

As a rider built into an annuity, the "use-it-or-lose-it" concept built into most traditional LTCI policies is often discarded.

Fixed index annuities with long-term care riders can be structured so a monthly or annual payout is increased by 150-200 percent for a certain period of time if two of the six activities of daily living cannot be performed by the policyholder.

One such example would be a $25,000 benefit from the annuity increased to $50,000 for a five-year period in which some type of long-term care, even home health care, is required. The additional payment is structured over a certain period of time, say five years, and then reverts to $25,000 again if the policy owner remains living.

CHAPTER 13

Mapping Your Legacy

"Give a man a fish and you feed him for a day; teach a man to fish and you feed him for a lifetime."

–Maimonides

Granted, we are not attorneys. So, as financial retirement professionals, we do not personally draw up wills or trusts, put together powers of attorney, or do anything requiring legal expertise.

However, we have multiple attorneys we consult with who can help with legal matters. Throughout the years, various challenges have been presented that could have been easily avoided with relatively simplistic maneuvering by an attorney.

A frank conversation regarding the inevitable may seem unpleasant, but it is certainly not unwarranted. Truth is, we are all mortal. We will all die. It is, quite simply, the final fact of life. Financially, death can create a heavy burden for those who have not planned properly.

Experiences can factor into someone's willingness to make arrangements for how to disperse assets and make plans to cope with death.

People who have dealt with the deaths of parents are often more inclined to resolve circumstances their own death could create. They have perhaps seen how the execution of proper estate planning simplified a process still made difficult because of the grief of losing a loved one. Or, they have perhaps seen an estate left to the whims and delays of probate because of minimal estate planning.

As part of the advice we dispense related to retirement planning, we certainly make every effort to be respectful when it comes to the wishes of clients in regard to their estates and their beneficiaries. Still, the discussion should not be dismissed.

****

One of the bigger dilemmas we encounter is the oversight that sometimes occurs when a client has moved to South Florida, making it their new permanent residence.

We had a couple, Ron and Marlou, who moved from the New England area after Ron sold his small business. They lived in New England for more than thirty years. Ron wore his Red Sox cap to the initial consultation, but when the couple left, I was convinced it was Marlou who knew enough about the Boston roster to qualify as one of those baseball statisticians who calculate advanced metrics.

Marlou and Ron had received investment advice for years from a big-box firm, but now they wanted a financial retirement plan and visited us based off a referral.

We were working on various matters while attempting to construct an income plan. Turns out, they had two homes in Florida after using one when they vacationed here. Now they profited from it as a vacation rental.

The two homes were, unsurprisingly, among Ron and Marlou's biggest assets. An estate attorney we are familiar with suggested to title the real estate into a trust. If a will is not constructed directing property into a trust at the time of the owner's death, the state in which you live may decide who should receive ownership of the property through probate, which can be a long, arduous exercise.

Ron and Marlou decided they needed a Florida domicile trust, which an attorney we consult with was happy to draw up for them at a discounted rate we helped negotiate. Maybe the money they saved on legal work can be used for a nice Red Sox banner somewhere in their home—just don't make reference to a "man cave" around Marlou.

Some of us in Florida call people (including Marlou and Ron) "snowbirds" when they live in a state farther north and come to Florida in the winter. Many snowbirds discover it is important to make sure all legal documentation has been updated to reflect their proper residency and make sure things are up to date, especially if they move to Florida permanently.

Important Considerations of Estate Planning

You will want to know about different documents for estate planning when establishing your legacy and while working with an attorney who specializes in estate planning.

Following are documents that could be part of that foundation:

POWERS OF ATTORNEY

This document provides someone the authority to act on your behalf, in your best interests. It is important to designate someone you trust to act on your behalf in situations where you cannot be present or have become incapacitated.

If, God forbid, you happen to be involved in a car accident that leaves you in a coma or suffering from some kind of head trauma for weeks, or even months, the bills you pay each month must still be reconciled. A power of attorney has the authority to pay your mortgage or cancel a service, such as cable.

You can authorize multiple powers of attorney to make decisions regarding different considerations. Two family members, perhaps a son and daughter, can be granted such authorization as joint powers of attorney. Both would then sign off on financial and business matters.

Different responsibilities can also be appointed to different POAs. That split could be made to designate someone who is most adept at health-related matters and someone who is most adept with financial issues. Each would have their own clearly defined roles as POAs.

In the case of health-related matters, it may be helpful to prepare an advanced medical directive. This document enables someone to outline choices made in advance regarding different health scenarios and how they are to be handled. An advanced medical directive can simplify difficult health-related decisions that tug at the hearts of family members, namely, end-of-life care.

Multiple powers of attorney can also act independently. As an example, picture a widowed mother. She enjoys visiting family in different parts of the country and routinely stays for extended periods with her children, appreciating them and all the things she can get out to do on her own. Each of her three children were named as independently authorized POAs, so the child closest to their mother, if something happened, could step in and act on her behalf.

WILLS

A will outlines your wishes for your estate and is perhaps the most basic legal document associated with estate planning. Basic, in this instance, also equates to necessary, since a will is the foundation of your legacy. It provides essential instructions detailing your desires and helps prevent any guesswork as to what becomes of your estate after you die.

That century-old dinner table and hutch that made your dining room a memorable place for the family to converse, relax, and play games may be something you promised a daughter who also made herself available to help with holiday gatherings. Because of her dedication, you may want her to have the table and hutch. Without a specific legal stipulation, however, it might go to an irresponsible son who pops in and out, if he comes at all, over the holidays.

It may not be enough to just have a will. Assets will be subject to probate, even if you have a will. Probate is the state's process for determining a will's validity. During probate, a judge will measure a will for timeliness, competence, and lawfulness. Also, the court will entertain any motions to contest the will, a process that can potentially take years to arbitrate and potentially escalates court costs and attorney's fees. Also, the process is public, which enables anyone to receive copies of the case, learn of your assets, and discover what is potentially being disputed and by whom.

A will can provide a more desirable probate process than intestacy (dying without a will). Not only are beneficiaries established and the distribution of property identified, but an executor can also be named to manage your estate.

A point of order worth noting in Florida:

State law requires a will be signed by the testator (the person who has made the will or given a legacy) or another person in the presence of the testator and under his direction. Two witnesses also must be present. Each of those witnesses must also sign the will. Florida does not require that a will be notarized. However, a "self-proving" will, which is usually more efficient because it enables the court to accept the will without contacting witnesses who signed it, requires notarization.

BENEFICIARIES

A precaution about the proper designation of beneficiaries is in order. One avoidable mistake, more common than you may believe, is the presence of someone who you no longer want as a beneficiary on a legal document.

For example, let's say the life insurance policy you took out ten, fifteen, maybe twenty years ago still contains your ex-spouse as a beneficiary. In spite of what is stipulated in your will, the company holding your insurance policy will still pay a benefit to your ex-spouse if that person is listed as a beneficiary.

Just ask yourself, "When was the last time I checked the beneficiary designations on documents?" The answer, if you're truthful with yourself, may be a bit shocking. Especially if you were recently divorced or remarried and suddenly realize, "I better check on this stuff." The same is true if a beneficiary dies. If that beneficiary was a sole beneficiary, and nothing was done to rename beneficiaries, the assets may undergo probate and the potentially costly and timely process it involves.

Sometimes, wills get changed to remove heirs (say, an ex-spouse or deceased relative), but beneficiary lines, which trump wills and last testaments, accidentally go unchanged. In such cases, an ex-spouse may receive the death benefit from a life insurance policy despite the deceased's wishes.

Realize, too, that any change in beneficiaries to a policy is the responsibility of the person who possesses the policy.

If mistakes are found, the process to change a beneficiary is usually quite simple and can be achieved with a simple form— sometimes it can even be handled online. More complicated beneficiary changes are often best resolved through the counsel of an estate attorney.

TRUSTS

Another legal document and part of a legacy plan is a trust, which allows a third party, or trustee, to hold your assets and determine how they will pass to your beneficiaries. A trust allows the trustee to hold assets and provide for a faster transfer of wealth while avoiding the expense, publicity, and time-consuming nature of probate.

Most importantly, perhaps, a trust can dictate greater control of your legacy and provide the peace of mind in knowing your estate will be managed in a manner you see fit.

This can be especially important if children are still minors, have a disability, or have a tendency to be wasteful of assets. Assets can be distributed to them based on time constraints established within the trust. If constructed properly by an attorney, your wishes in these and other matters should withstand any challenges, unlike easily contested wills.

Consideration must be given to the nature of the trust. A revocable trust enables you to change terms while you are alive. An irrevocable trust allows you no recourse to change terms, and you no longer have control of the contents.

Tax benefits to irrevocable trusts are more substantial but remain subject to a Medicaid look-back period. So, if you transfer your assets into an irrevocable trust in an attempt to shelter them from a Medicaid spend-down, you will be ineligible for Medicaid coverage for long-term care for five years. Still, probate and estate taxes can be avoided with an irrevocable trust, which can potentially protect assets from legal judgments against you.

You must remember to fund a trust, retitling assets to the trust. A competent estate attorney should see to this, but it is worth noting so you, too, are aware of what could become a costly oversight.

From Here to There: Value a Second Opinion

"We are all in the same boat in a stormy sea, and we owe each other a terrible loyalty."

–G. K. Chesterson

The vast majority of the people with whom we meet are committed to principles that have allowed them to save money. Consequently, they are aware of the discipline involved with building their wealth. In addition, they have previous experiences with financial investment advisors from which they can compare and contrast their first meeting with us. They usually feel somewhat relaxed and are not overly fearful of some unexpected revelation we might share after putting their portfolio through an initial stress test.

With them, we hope to establish a quick rapport. The meetings we conduct attempt to spare prospective clients of embarrassment or frustration.

Our goal is for people to walk out of our office and say, "They don't only care about our money! They also care about *us!*"

We attempt to gain an understanding of the prospective client by listening. We want to hear everything that is going on in their lives and blend that with their goals and their vision for retirement. Our business is about people, first and foremost. Only after establishing that priority can we attempt to make the numbers work for our clients.

Interests Vary; Retirement Plans Do, Too

Virtually anything goes in our community, where the weather is warm and retirees treasure a life well-lived . . . especially when life no longer requires them to work.

We are located near a broad expanse of water, the Atlantic Ocean. We love to boat and are big into water sports. We also fish and know many of our clients enjoy similar interests, though the activities they are engaged in run the gamut. Often, those activities—travel, for instance—require detailed calculations.

Obviously, we have to ask questions and have become skilled at doing so based on needs we have incorporated into retirement plans. Sometimes, we phrase questions differently to get answers pertaining to specific retirement goals and to gain a full understanding of the lives people lead.

No worthwhile recommendations can be made, no valuable feedback offered, until it becomes clear what someone is doing, what they want from their retirement, and what the point is to all this money they have accumulated. Their personal and financial goals illuminate what is most important about their money.

To varying degrees, people come into our office, hear the questions asked in the initial consultation, and seemingly sense they are in a completely different meeting than any conducted by their previous financial advisor.

Those who have been with captive advisors representing big-box financial firms sometimes feel as if they've been sold financial instruments and don't feel as if they ever had much of a relationship with their advisor. Maybe questions weren't regularly asked. Maybe meetings weren't regularly scheduled. Whatever the case, the relationship seemed impersonal and the advisor seemed disinterested.

We want them to sense they are with a firm that wants to prepare a conservative financial plan for the rest of their lives, including retirement. Often, the approach is a refreshing change for them if they became accustomed to a financial advisor who tries to sell them on this or that.

Personalities differ. Some may be more hesitant than others to reveal their life's ambitions. We understand this, which is why we strive to remind prospective clients their first meeting with us is a no-cost, no-obligation venture in which they are receiving a viewpoint regarding their portfolio.

We start off with the assumption, and the expectation, that whatever someone is spending now is sustainable in retirement. We would all rather avoid big changes in spending habits. Once an average monthly expense is established, we look into all sources of income to determine if this level is possible to maintain in retirement without a major lifestyle change.

Quite often, that's possible. The aspiring retiree has saved enough and is not spending in a carefree manner, and their lifestyle is sustainable.

Sometimes, however, things are not as rosy. A tough conversation is necessary to convince someone changes in spending habits are necessary if they are going to make their savings last through retirement.

Greg and Natalie: Letting Go of the Fear

Greg and Natalie were a warm, vibrant couple who entered our office one day wanting to prepare for retirement.

This seemingly simple step can be a monumental breakthrough. For whatever reason, people simply put off planning for retirement. Why? Well, there are many reasons.

Fear is one of them. Fear of the unknown. Fear of realizing they may not have enough money saved. Fear they are not on the right track. Fear of consulting with a financial advisor because they do not want to get sidetracked by a pushy salesman and tricked into a risky investment. Fear of whether a financial advisor they do not know can be trusted with their life savings.

Fear, quite frankly, of retirement, and fear of all that goes into the execution of a broad-based plan.

An adage in our industry is people often spend more time planning vacations than they do retirement. Maybe that's because vacation, while often framed as a brief adventure, is condensed into a short time frame and, depending on what you want to do, can be researched rather easily.

The length of retirement, meanwhile, cannot be easily defined, though once you commit, it entails every moment for the rest of your life. Hardly a short-term objective. At least, let's hope not.

People cannot easily envision how long they will live. In addition, retirement is loaded with variables, some of which are difficult to predict (think health issues) in terms of severity and longevity.

Yet, Greg and Natalie made the right move in walking through our doors. They were aware of how much they had saved in their retirement accounts and were eager to implement a plan to help them prepare for their golden years. They realized retirement should not be a do-it-yourself project.

Greg was a dermatologist, Natalie a stay-at-home mom. They had saved close to $2 million for retirement. They were in their mid-fifties and grappling with expenses incurred by their two children, who were both in college.

Their over-arching question was typical. Were they on the right path?

Could their savings enable Greg and Natalie to live the kind of lifestyle they wanted to maintain in retirement? They were already seeing an advisor, though he was really a broker who was looking to make Greg considerable money in the market. In turn, the investments allowed the broker to profit off products he was captive to selling for his firm.

Not all advisors who essentially fulfill a role as broker are unsavory. In the case of Greg and Natalie, they found their financial advisor to be pleasant enough and were pleased with how their retirement accounts had progressed. But, they sensed a broader outlook was needed.

Good thing they did.

The risk analysis we conduct is customized to consider variables specific to each individual or couple. Greg and Natalie were a bit shocked by their risk assessment. They informed us they did not want to lose any more than 10 percent of their portfolio if their funds were subjected to a market correction. We discovered, based on the level of risk in their accounts, they could stand to lose close to 30 percent if the market tumbled.

Actually, that's not at all unusual. Sometimes the percentage is much higher. People move along, focused on their daily routines, thinking their investments are relatively conservative. Risk analysis, however, determines they could lose 40 percent of their savings in a market correction. Maybe more. *Gulp.*

Another discovery was perhaps even more alarming to Greg and Natalie. When we analyzed the costs of their investments, they were paying more than 2.5 percent a year in fees. When they learned this, they weren't so happy with their guy from the big-box firm, who they had thought was squarely in their corner.

We wanted them to reconsider their investments—one, so they weren't paying as much in fees; two, so they had more choices an independent firm like ours is able to offer; and three, to also reduce the risk inherent in their current market allocation.

Even with a lower return on their savings, Greg and Natalie could visualize a situation where they were going to be okay as long as they adapted to a process they were willing to follow.

Retirement Dilemma: Finding Occupation…for Your Time

Be aware that retirement represents a stark change in how you spend your days and your time—to the extent that some advisors even tell clients to take time off from work and then spend their days based on how they envision them in retirement.

This, however, seems kind of silly.

If you're still employed and are paid vacation benefits, the time you take off is considered vacation. You will spend it with the mindset you are able to take a break from work, and, if lucky, not even think about your job. But, your job still exists. You will go back to it. Rather quickly, in fact.

In retirement (assuming you are fully retired), there is no job and, thus, no pending return to work. The first few weeks are delightful. You might even relax and spend them like you typically spent a "stay-cation." In time, however, that feeling wears off.

The view from the deck grows familiar. The shows on TV become dull. The walls of the house close tighter. You gain a complete realization you're growing old. Your days, if they have been spent idly with very little to do, become tedious. You find yourself unfulfilled and bored.

We have actually had clients ask us if there was something, anything, they could do around our office.

One client was a banker accustomed to not only a full day at the office, but also serviceable and charitable events that filled his time on weeknights and even weekends. He resorted to testing his skills as a handyman while knowing his craftsmanship was limited.

He looked for anything he could find around the house that was in need of the slightest repair or update. He resorted to spending time many days browsing the aisles of home improvement stores. Or, he would look in the fridge, find it was missing a few items, jot down a list, and head to the grocery store to push a cart up and down every aisle. He looked like a consumer, but what he was really doing was consuming time.

Eventually, we hope this client finds his footing and can embrace a hobby, something we strongly recommend to all our aspiring retirees.

You Can Aspire to Inspire in Retirement

Some of the activities other clients have engaged in during retirement *actually inspired us* to want to be more active.

Paula spent her career as a grade school teacher and was single. She recognized soon after retirement that twenty-four hours in a day can drag on incessantly without anything to do or look forward to.

Although Paula was a long lover of trails and enjoyed taking in nature, serious hiking had never been a pastime during her summers off. Once she began walking on a regular basis, however, she sensed she was fit enough to go hiking. Her interest in that pursuit has escalated to the point where, at least twice each year, she goes on lengthy hikes with others who arrive at the same trailhead from all parts of the country. Throughout the year, Paula stays in touch with her hiking friends through social media and, on occasion, renews acquaintances through social events.

Days as a teacher can be quite lengthy. Papers to grade, lesson plans to prepare, and parents to consult left little time for Paula to engage in a regular exercise regimen. Now, she feels as fit as she did in college and her retirement rarely finds her lounging.

Retirement is a journey. Paula took that concept an extra step—well, many a step—and literally discovered new paths with new people to satisfy her journey.

It's proof: Retirement can be what you make of it.

About the Author:
C. Grant Conness

The day Grant turned fifteen, he understood he was old enough to join the Fort Lauderdale workforce.

Encouraged by the prospect of earning his own income, Grant got on his bicycle and rode to Bravo Italiano, a longtime staple among local restaurants. He was hired on the spot, given an apron, and told to bus tables.

Not that Grant didn't have other things to do. As a football player, he would become a budding college prospect who eventually played for a national championship team. As a bandsman, he continually practiced at playing the bass guitar and eventually toured as part of a national act.

While these endeavors, as well as his first job in the financial services industry, took Grant out of Florida, the connections he made growing up and the fondness he maintained for his hometown eventually led Grant to raise his family in Fort Lauderdale, which is home to Global Wealth Management.

Grant's passions include boating, surfing, and paddle-boarding. He is an avid sports fan who attends a variety of Miami sports events.

Grant enjoys spending time with his wife Jessica, and their four children: Kirra, Kylie, Kinley, and Cody. One of Grant's favorite pursuits has been coaching youth teams involving each of his kids.

Community projects and charities Grant supports include Feeding South Florida, The Jason Taylor Foundation, OneBlood, Racing For Cancer, and Women In Distress.

Grant, a registered Investment Adviser Representative held to a fiduciary standard, is a co-host of *The Global Wealth Show*, which airs on both radio and television. As a recognized professional in the financial services industry, he has contributed articles for *Kiplinger* and been quoted in major publications such as *The Wall Street Journal*, *USA Today*, and *Newsweek*. He has appeared on major television networks such as CBS, NBC, ABC, and FOX.

> *"I was born and raised right here in South Florida. I grew up in Fort Lauderdale. My oldest daughter started her first year in college when my youngest was starting in grade school. We have a nice age range there, and it fuels my passion for what I do in my personal life. It's great also seeing Global Wealth Management grow in a community I've loved all my life."*
> —C. Grant Conness

About the Author:
Andrew M. Costa

Some of Andrew's favorite memories as a kid are from attending Miami Hurricanes football games with his father. The Hurricanes were not just any college program in the 1980s. Coached by Howard Schnellenberger and Jimmy Johnson, Miami captured two national championships. Although the program happily embraced a renegade image, one relatively simple and innocuous hand gesture—a "U" sign—became the universal symbol and nickname for the university and its football image.

Andrew grew up with all of that while rooting on the likes of Bernie Kosar, Vinny Testaverde, Michael Irvin, Warren Sapp, and Ray Lewis. Andrew's allegiance did not waver, even while attending Florida State, one of the Hurricanes' bitter rivals within a state loaded with great football. While Andrew cherished the educational and social opportunities presented in Tallahassee, he forever remained loyal to the beloved 'Canes.

That allegiance remains one of many that endears Andrew to the Miami area and his hometown of Fort Lauderdale, which is home to Global Wealth Management. In addition to his love for Miami sports teams, both college and pro, Andrew's passions include golf, boating, and sail fishing.

He also loves to travel, especially when you count a day spent enjoying the short trip to Bimini and the clear, blue waters that make the Atlantic Ocean passage a favorite for boaters.

Andrew cherishes time spent with his boys, Austin and Dylan, while keeping up with their many activities.

Community projects and charities Andrew supports include the Salvation Army, Petset—Humane Society of Broward County, Racing For Cancer, Women In Distress, and Kids In Distress.

Andrew, a Registered Representative, is a co-host of *The Global Wealth Show,* which airs on both radio and television. As a recognized professional in the financial services industry, he has contributed articles for *Kiplinger* and been quoted in major publications such as *The Wall Street Journal, USA Today,* and *Newsweek.* He has appeared on major television networks such as CBS, NBC, ABC, and FOX.

> *"Fort Lauderdale is definitely home. I couldn't imagine really living anywhere else. It's sort of a paradise. It's a community I take pride in. Just being the financial advisory firm we've grown to be at Global Wealth Management, it's awesome so many people know of us and have really good things to say. It's just a really neat deal."*
>
> *— Andrew Costa*

GWM With Purpose

We both grew up in Fort Lauderdale and have found it rewarding to grow Global Wealth Management into a financial practice that has helped so many families in South Florida with retirement planning.

Our business is much like a family, too. As such, the team at GWM is honored and humbled to help with charitable endeavors in our community. Associates with Global Wealth Management engage in numerous projects. We also encourage our clients to participate in charitable endeavors GWM is associated with. Many clients have become regulars helping with charities and have told us their commitment has provided them greater purpose in retirement.

We have forged relationships with several local charities, including the following:

JASON TAYLOR FOUNDATION

The mission of the Jason Taylor Foundation is to support and create programs that facilitate the personal growth and empowerment of South Florida's children in need by focusing on improved health care, education, and quality of life.

The Foundation was founded in July 2004 by Jason Taylor, a defensive end for the Miami Dolphins who was elected to the Pro Football Hall of Fame and was also named the 2007 NFL Man of the Year.

Since opening its doors, the Jason Taylor Foundation has contributed almost $6 million to youth programs and services. With Jason's commitment and the continued support of community members and civic leaders, the Jason Taylor

Foundation works tirelessly to achieve its goal of building better futures for the youth of South Florida.

Members of the Global Wealth Management team participate each year in JT's Ping Pong Smash, which pairs local celebrities from sports and entertainment with generous community members in a doubles table tennis tournament. We are both dedicated fathers and passionate about sports. The event is a great way to interact in a fun and competitive environment.

RACING FOR CANCER

Ryan Hunter Reay, a client of Global Wealth Management and a good friend of Andrew's, was the 2012 winner of the Indianapolis 500. That same year Ryan captured the Indy Car Series championship.

Racing For Cancer is the non-profit organization founded by Ryan Hunter Reay in 2009 after his mother passed away after fighting cancer.

The charity focuses its efforts on early detection and prevention, while also helping fight childhood cancer. Racing For Cancer, through its corporate matching partner, AutoNation, has donated more than $4 million since 2010. The charity has adopted the motto, "Helping Pick Up the Pace . . . One Fan at a Time!"

FEEDING SOUTH FLORIDA

Each year, Global Wealth Management organizes a food drive. GWM clients and staff have contributed more than 1,000 pounds of food to this worthwhile cause. The team at GWM has also donated time to pack food boxes distributed by Feeding South Florida. The food banks serve Palm Beach, Broward, Miami-Dade, and Monroe counties.

More than 98 percent of all financial donations to Feeding South Florida aid those in each of the counties served. Every dollar donated can provide six meals for those in need.

Through direct-service programs and a network of nonprofit partner agencies, including soup kitchens, food pantries, homeless shelters, and day cares, Feeding South Florida processes 44 million pounds of food per year, as well as leading hunger and poverty advocacy efforts and providing innovative programming and education.

KIDS IN DISTRESS

Global Wealth Management sponsors an annual toy drive to provide donations to this charity. Hundreds of toys are purchased and donated by GWM clients and staff to Kids In Distress, a nationally accredited agency working for the prevention of child abuse, preservation of the family, and the treatment of abused and neglected children.

GWM staff members also choose a day out of the year to volunteer with the KID organization and spend time interacting and playing games with children in the program.

The five-acre Leo Goodwin Campus in Broward County, as well as a satellite office in Palm Beach County, offer community-based programs focused on prevention, intervention, foster care, and family counseling. Educational programs have also been developed in the KID preschool and aftercare settings.

WOMEN IN DISTRESS

Clothing drives have been arranged by Global Wealth Management, which enable clients and staff to help Women In Distress through donations of gently used garments. Women In Distress is the only full-service domestic violence center in Broward County that is nationally accredited and state certified.

The mission of Women In Distress is to stop domestic violence abuse for everyone through intervention, education, and advocacy. The center offers twenty-four-hour crisis intervention through its hotline and emergency shelter, as well as counseling and support for victims and their children.

ONEBLOOD

Global Wealth Management has encouraged clients and staff to participate in community blood drives. As part of that effort, the Big Red Bus belonging to OneBlood has parked outside our Fort Lauderdale office to provide a convenient location for clients and staff to donate blood.

OneBlood is a not-for-profit community organization responsible for providing safe, available, and affordable blood to more than 200 hospital partners throughout most of Florida. It distributes one million products annually, employs more than 2,000 people, operates more than eighty donor centers, and deploys nearly 200 signature Big Red Buses to service areas for blood drives.

www.ingramcontent.com/pod-product-compliance
Lightning Source LLC
Chambersburg PA
CBHW070817160726
48004CB00001B/311